# Women in Media Careers

*Success Despite the Odds*

**Lee Bollinger and Carole O'Neill**

**University Press of America,® Inc.**
Lanham · Boulder · New York · Toronto · Plymouth, UK

Copyright © 2008 by
University Press of America,® Inc.
4501 Forbes Boulevard
Suite 200
Lanham, Maryland 20706
UPA Acquisitions Department (301) 459-3366

Estover Road
Plymouth PL6 7PY
United Kingdom

Library of Congress Control Number: 2008929745
ISBN-13: 978-0-7618-4133-3 (paperback : alk. paper)
ISBN-10: 0-7618-4133-4 (paperback : alk. paper)
eISBN-13: 978-0-7618-4218-7
eISBN-10: 0-7618-4218-7

Cover photos: top, Sue Ann Staake-Wayne, directing from
CBS control room, Washington, DC; bottom, Carolyn Murray
and Gwen Fowler, senior editors reviewing the daily paper
at The Sun News, Myrtle Beach, SC.

# Contents

# Preface

This text introduces the reader to the genres and careers of mass communication outlets (books, newspapers, radio, movies, magazines, television) as well as the newest of mass media, the internet. However, the main focus is on women who opt for careers in mass media, their efforts in breaking through glass ceilings, and their success in obtaining levels of executive power, *despite the odds*. The reader will learn about the differences in career successes (clout positions and salaries) of women who work in print media (books, newspapers and magazines) and those who obtain careers in visual media (broadcast and film). The text also offers tips for breaking into careers in mass media outlets. The text does not focus on women's issues and media, *per se*, but the subject of gender inequality at top levels of media companies is covered with factual data. Still, the authors point out that while corporate disparity exists in media careers, the gap is narrowing, and, compared to the rest of corporate America, women have more success in climbing media career ladders.

Again, we acknowledge gender inequality and glass ceilings in media-related venues, which can be backed up with data. Our central argument is that while women can see the top of the corporate ladder in media companies, they indeed find it very difficult if not impossible to get to the CEO-Executive levels of parent companies. However, the glass ceiling has become more and more penetrable especially with vibrant changes taking place since 1999 with respect to women in certain management levels of mass media. We also note extraordinary women, media divas, who succeed in more than one mass medium, and those who go beyond their boundaries, succeed in multiple genres of media or entertainment, and break any and all glass ceilings in their way, that we call *diversified divas*. We think the uniqueness here is that our divas are females who have succeeded in using their names as "brands," like Madonna, Martha,

Christina and Oprah, for example. A section in each chapter, an entire chapter and an appendix are devoted to these divas.

Finally, when gathering facts, statistics and latest trends about any topic, especially mass media, one risks publishing material that has already changed by the time a text goes into print. The mass media, as an industry, are dynamic, which means ever-changing. In both print and electronic media, people are always moving from one position into another. In fact, like we have told our students, if one wishes to venture into the news media or entertainment media, one had better forego significant relationships and expect to move around quite a bit in the first 10 years. Several of our students have gone off into the abyss of either television, newspapers or movie industry, and over the last several years we have found it impossible to keep up with them. We stay in contact if they keep in touch with us.

Any venue under the heading of mass media is highly competitive, and the higher one climbs the more competitive it gets. In other words, it's a tough business.

# Acknowledgments

W e owe much thanks to some researchers who have helped us: Kristy Goodall, who was an English major at the university when Lee first conceived of the idea of this text; Whitney Howard who helped us out on Media Divas, and Ashley Cyr who is doing research as we write this on the media conglomerates. Carole is especially grateful to Kate Sedrowski for her dedication and determination to research and interview women in entertainment in order to complete her senior thesis documentary, Because I Am A Woman. Carole's former graduate assistant, Amanda Treat was helpful with early research into the world of Divas.

Both authors would like to thank their female students who have had an ongoing interest in media careers. They hope that this book will answer some of the concerns they have in venturing out after graduation into the male dominated clout positions in the media world.

Lastly, we can't forget all our female friends working in the media who have not let anything like *a glass ceil*ing daunt their progress.

# Chapter One

# Women's Careers in Media

While women today have jobs in all of mass media, the 1950s may be long remembered as the worst decade for women in the media industry. Jobs in media (broadcast and print) were more and more difficult to get and hold, and women in these jobs endured biased treatment. Mostly, women were relegated to jobs that were *assistants* to copywriters, copy editors, program directors, and sales directors or managers. Women in all genres of media were repressed or misrepresented, and women workers were still the minority in general.

Then, by 1965, women workers numbered 33.4 percent of the work force. Women were heading toward careers. Women working in various mass media jobs now numbered 85,000. In 1992, 45.3 percent of all women worked, and 32.28 percent of media-related jobs were held by women; by 2000, 46.4 percent of all women worked, and women held 41.4 percent in media-related jobs. According to figures released by the Bureau of Labor Statistics (BLS) (for 2004), 59.5 percent of all women worked, and 46.6 percent of media-related jobs were held by women. For 2005, BLS disclosed 56.2 percent of jobs were held by women, and in the nearly six million media-related jobs,[1] 46 percent were held by women. While the ratio of 54 percent men and 46 percnt women in media-related jobs is almost the same as the ratio for all jobs in 2006 held by women in America (Table 1.1), there is apparently unequal career opportunity in mass media across America for women in general at the very top level of management that we speculate is indicative of all corporate level jobs in this country.

Women, overall, held under 50 percent of all key positions connected with mass media and media providers, such as advertising, in

2004 (See Table 2.3 appended to Chapter 2). Reaching for higher positions, such as program director, for example, and not obtaining it because of one's gender is an example of a glass ceiling firmly in place. However, as we show in this text, women continue to obtain "clout" positions, like program director (television and radio), producer (film, television and radio), publisher (books and newspapers), despite the fact that in the very top levels, the CEO's, Executive Governance and Boards of Directors, white men still dominate. Being aware of the success of such women makes one appreciate them more. What does it take to become aware? First, it takes media literacy.

# Media Literacy, Mass Media
# v. Mass Communication

Becoming more media-literate enables people to objectively and intelligently respond better to images and ratios that may seem unfair. According to Art Silverblatt, media literacy is a means of analysis of information for specific outcomes.[2] The Center for Media Literacy, a nonprofit educational organization under IRS 501(c)3, states on its WEB page the following:

> The Center for Media Literacy is dedicated to a new vision of literacy for the 21st Century: the ability to communicate competently in all media forms, print and electronic, as well as to access, understand, analyze and evaluate the powerful images, words and sounds that make up our contemporary mass media culture.[3]

Media literacy then incorporates elements of being aware of the impact of media messages on the individual and society, having an understanding of the process of mass communication in general, being able to develop strategies with which to analyze and discuss media messages and having an awareness of media content as "text" material, thereby enhancing the cultivation of enjoyment. Being *media literate* means one has a fairly good understanding of mass media, which differs from the term, *mass communication.*

**Mass communication** applies to any **means** by which one communicates with masses of people. A magazine is a means of mass communication; it is also a category or genre of mass media. The two words, "mass media" and "mass communication" are often exchanged for each other but actually in context mean entirely different things.

When we talk about mass communicating with people, we are implying that we use mass media to do so. Also, mass communication can be spoken about as a discipline; hence, one can study mass communication. (A problem arises when we put an "s" on the word "communication" for, then, one means information systems, such as telephones, satellite or cable systems).

At times, one term is used for the other; one might say "I want to pursue a career in mass communication " when what the speaker means is "I want to pursue a career in mass media.

**Mass media,** then, applies collectively to all the entities (channels or vehicles) that are used to communicate with the masses or mass audiences. Each *medium* of communication reaches a "mass" audience, as opposed to a personal message to an individual. The word, "mass," applies to many people as a whole. The word, "media," is plural for the word "medium." The newspaper is a medium; magazine as a form of communication is a medium; television is an electronic medium, as is radio.

For the sake of easing things a bit about the terms, let's differentiate them this way in formal definitions:

> **Media literacy** is the ability to access and analyze messages in mass media.
>
> **Mass communication** is the method by which we develop messages of all types to deliver to large and very diverse audiences through mass media channels.
>
> **Mass media** are the venues, the genres, used for the distribution of mass communication messages and include newspapers, magazines, books, movies, television, radio and the internet.

# Media Divas and Beyond

While there have been hundreds of women working in radio and television since the 1960s, nearly all of the officers and district managers of the National Association of Broadcasters, as well as executives of the other important broadcasting organizations and the executives at the publishing companies, have been men. At the networks, the decision-makers were all male also.[4] Clearly, a glass ceiling has been firmly in place; that is, a ceiling that can be seen but not touched. It meant that while women could see the top positions, the glass ceiling was impossible to break.

Yet, women obtained jobs in book, newspaper and magazine publishing, and in film, television and radio industries. And women continue to succeed into higher positions, especially in the film and television industries. Some women who make it big in one genre, like film, and who have the acumen for business quickly jump into other media capitalizing on their names. We call these women "media divas."

Rather than settling for success in one genre of mass media, some women diversify. By this, we mean that some women know the business strategy of building careers in more than one medium, of creating themselves as a "brand." Oprah Winfrey, on the other hand, is one clear example of what we call a *Diversified Diva* because she has been able to navigate from television reporter to movie star, from show host to magazine publisher, and more recently to Broadway producer (*The Color of Purple*) and has remained concentrated as a brand in media. Even her production company, Harpo Productions (Oprah spelled backwards), is a media company. Also, there are *MultiMedia Divas*; these divas cross media lines but remain in mass media. One such example is Lucille Ball, who went from radio to film to television to owner of Desilu Productions. There are many such *divas* in media and we highlight them as we move through the text. In Chapter Ten, we explain the concept of the media diva in detail.

What is important to remember about these divas is that they, by branding their names, succeed in shattering the media glass ceilings in their path.

# Summary

There is an obvious under-representation of women in top level positions in parent companies that encompass mass media today. This, however, is contrary to the fact that women are fully represented in clout positions—women with power in media, perhaps more so in the visual media of film and television. To do an evaluation of where women fit within media careers, one must explore each genre (medium) of mass media outlets, determine who is in authority positions and where women are working within the power structure of that medium. Being media literate and understanding the difference between mass communication and mass media help people better discern media messages. In understanding the concept of the glass ceiling, we point toward celebrity women (divas) and how they break traditions.

Careers for women in media are explored in each chapter in more detail. In the next chapter, Chapter 2, we discuss the glass ceiling.

*Table 1.1. U.S. Civilian Labor Force 1950-2004*

| Years | 1950 | 1960 | 1970 | 1980 | 1990 | 2000 | 2004 June | 2006 May |
|---|---|---|---|---|---|---|---|---|
| Percents | | | | | | | | |
| Men | 70.4 | 66.6 | 61.9 | 57.5 | 54.7 | 74.5 | 76.1 | 70.1 |
| Women | 33.4 | 33.4 | 38.1 | 42.5 | 45.3 | 60.0 | 59.5 | 56.6 |

From The American Work Force, 1992-2005, Monthly Labor Review.

# Notes

1. Defined by BLS under two categories: (1) Arts, Design, Entertainment, Sports and Media Occupations, and (2) Information. We deduct the more than 200,000 jobs in the sports category that includes coaches, athletes, and related workers and include 12,000 women in computer and mathematical (systems) occupations and the 32,000 women in advertising and promotions managers category.

2. Art Silverblatt. *Media Literacy: Keys to Interpreting Media Messages.* (Westport, Ct: Praeger, 1995), p. 2.

3. Center for Media Literacy, Vision, at www.medialit.org.

4. Halper, p. 189.

# Chapter Two

# The Glass Ceiling, as Metaphor

Met•a•phor—a figure of speech in which a word ordinarily meaning one thing is actually designated to mean another thing, e.g., *the world is a stage and we are players on it,* is credited as Shakespeare's and used often. It literally means that if one sees the world through the backdrop of theater, one could see a huge stage (the planet) with actors on it. The metaphor then has broader meanings about people in general, acting out scenes called life.

Women consistently have struggled in corporate America; climbing the career ladder has meant breaking through or busting through glass ceilings—*those invisible barriers that one can see through but not easily get through.* Various scholars have dedicated large amounts of time tracking women's progress [discussed below] and commissions on government levels have been formed over the last 10 years to search for answers [also discussed below]. Meanwhile, in mass media, women continue to survive and actually thrive in their career choices. Men (most are Caucasian) are still holding onto the top positions, e.g., Rupert Murdoch (News Corp. that owns FOX); Sumner Redstone (Sumner Redstone, Exec. Chairman of the Board of Viacom (that owns Paramount) and Chairman of the Board of CBS Corporation); Jeffrey Immelt (CEO of GE that owns 80% of NBC/Universal Studios); Richard Parsons (CEO of Time Warner that owns Warner Studios and the Turner Cable System); Robert Iger (CEO of Disney that owns film companies, music outlets, cable stations and theme parks); Sir Howard Stringer (CEO of Sony Pictures).

Sony Corporation owns Columbia TriStar and other film companies as well as Sony Pictures Television, Sony BMG Music [half-owned by

Bertelsmann]; and Bertelsmann AG, a European company has six divisions that include European TV channels, radio stations, television production, music publishing companies, online media e-commerce, as well as magazines, periodicals, newspapers and book publishing, such as Bantam Books, Doubleday, Random, Knopf and many others (see Table 2.1). The six divisions of Bertelsmann are controlled, [CEOS], again by "white" men; Liz Mohn, wife to the Chairman Emeritus, Reinhard Mohn, of Bertelsmann AG's Supervisory Board, was recently a front-runner for CEO of the AG; in the end Gunter Thielen was appointed. The ratio of women on the corporate executive levels in the top news/entertainment conglomerate mega-corporations amount to 13 percent on the Boards of Directors and 16 percent on the executive levels of management (see Table 2.1). However, while the top level positions are of concern in this paper, it is what women have been doing below the glass ceiling that is notable and of more concern to us. Also, we, the researchers, offer a theoretical perspective about the steadfastness of the glass ceiling that may shed light on the length of time it is taking women to climb beyond any barriers.

## Below Corporate Ceilings, Above the Crowd

There is a slight dichotomy in careers for women in mass media. Women in the entertainment industry (film and television) are becoming more and more the movers and shakers of production, and women in magazines and newspapers, although struggling with the print industry in general, are still lagging in power positions. In the 2006 issue of *Fortune*, Cathleen Black, President of Hearst Magazines, Ann Moore, CEO of Time Inc. [just recently Nora McAniff resigned as co-chief operating officer who is nearing her 25 year anniversary with Time; also Sylvia Auton was recently appointed Executive Vice President at Time], and Oprah Winfrey, CEO of Harpo Productions are in the top six.[1] In an October 11, 2006 article by Patricia Sellers, Fortune editor-at-large, Viacom and other entertainment outlets are named with women in the powerful position seats: MTV Networks CEO Judy McGrath; Nickelodeon Chief Cyma Zarghami; BET Networks boss Debra Lee; Paramount Pictures former president, Gail Berman, and Paramount owes to its credit for past employment positions, Anne Sweeney (now at Walt Disney) and Sherry Lansing, Retired Paramount Chair. Other power seats are Oxygen Media CEO Geraldine Laybourne and Lifetime Entertainment Services CEO Betty Cohen; as well as Stacey Snider, at DreamWorks SKG (a recent acquisition of Viacom's).[2]

In the newspaper industry, women publishers continue to increase. Northwestern University looked at 137 daily newspapers with a circulation of more than 85,000 in 2003[3] and found that 18% had female publishers; editors likewise continue to increase. Gannett Co. (owner of 94 newspapers) reported in 2002 that 25 papers were run by female [publishers]. The Tribune Co.'s 10 daily newspapers [includes Chicago Tribune] has four women publishers. McClatchy Company, which owned 11 daily newspapers in 2003 then purchased 12 Knight-Ridder newspapers, has a one-third ratio of women in executive positions; formerly, one-half of its 11 daily newspapers had female publishers. With the Knight-Ridder purchase, that ratio is about one-third (see Table 2.2). (Sheila Gibbons, Media Report to Women, however, reported that 64.5 percent of all supervisors in newsrooms are men as well as 60 percent of all reporters).[4]

The position of publisher is the highest paid position at a newspaper, daily or otherwise. Most daily newspapers are part of large conglomerates (viz.a.viz, McClatchy-Knight-Ridder, Hearst, Gannett [the largest]), so all publishers report to corporate officers. It is the same with the entertainment industry [and the researchers purposely include television where news is more entertainment format than informative format]; the top levels of the big companies (mentioned earlier) are still in control but the bottom-line—who makes money for the company—controls the purse strings. A list of important and powerful women in news and entertainment is appended (end of chapter) as a sample. Nevertheless, the researchers do not claim the glass ceiling has disappeared but rather that it is still quite valid, just seemingly at times more like clear jello than glass in media careers. Before making theoretical connections about the slow progress made in careers for women in general, the glass ceiling and media careers are explored.

## Glass Ceiling Defined

The first reference for the term, "glass ceiling," may be attributed to Gay Bryant, then editor of *Working Woman*, who in an interview is quoted as saying, "Women have reached a certain point—I call it the glass ceiling. They're in the top of middle management and they're stopping and getting stuck."[5]

In 1991, the U.S. Labor Secretary, Lynn Martin, released findings entitled, "The Glass Ceiling Initiative" which had examined an obvious lack of women and minorities in management across all jobs.

In this report, the glass ceiling was defined as:

> those artificial barriers based on attitudinal or organizational bias that prevent qualified individuals from advancing upward in their organization into management-level positions (p. 1).[6]

In 1994, Donald Tomukorie-Devey, then Professor of Sociology at North Carolina State University, chaired a Glass Ceiling Commission report for the U.S. Department of Labor. In the report, he explained why the glass ceiling was in place:

> The higher one rises in a managerial or professional hierarchy the more likely the future promotions are based on trust, social similarity and access to the informal networks of power and influence in the organizations. Women and minorities are particularly disadvantaged on these dimensions in many work places. It is far easier to integrate lower levels of management than it is to crack glass ceilings.[7]

The glass ceiling then is a workplace bias based on attitudes/dispositions toward gender and class as well as unwritten cultural (social) norms within organizations. If women (and minority men as well) are limited in their ability to become members of certain social clubs and/or gain access to places where they can form networks with people in power, then naturally there will be limits in much of their career mobility. How strongly the metaphor applies to national mass media is our research question for this chapter.

## Media Careers and Wages/Positions

Even with the Equal Pay Act, 2003 data reveal a continued wage gap based on gender and race, which indicates that all women in race categories were lagging in equal pay at 75.6 cents per every $1.00 men earned (both Black and Hispanic men) (See Table 2.2).

Clara Jeffery, an editor of *Mother Jones* magazine, reported in 2006 that women were then making 80 cents on the male $1.00, that over her career the average working woman loses $1.2 million to wage inequity, and that since 1963, when the Equal Pay Act was signed, the wage gap has closed by less than half a cent per year.[8]

Equally, then, or dollar for dollar, women continue to earn less than men. According to the U.S. Department of Labor's Women's Bureau site, the bureau was established in 1920 "to represent the needs of wage-earning women in the public policy process," and while the bureau claims to be a "champion for the interests of women's work," no reports in their archives mention the glass ceiling metaphor. Also, the publications seem to focus on just a few occupations but not the media industry, *per se*.

Most of the media careers-for-women sites that do focus on wage disparity and the metaphor of the glass ceiling began in the 1990s, e.g., Women's eNews, Catalyst, and DataLine. Women eNews (2002) focuses on news that concerns women and public policies and articles about women in media careers are published often.[9] Catalyst is a research and advisory services organization and a nonprofit since 1997; it regularly focuses on women in corporate management (in the Fortune 500 companies), publishing quantitative and qualitative findings.[10] Data Line (1991) was created as a newsletter to report on the glass ceiling in American corporations.[11]

Additional data are available at these locations: Equal Employment Occupation Commission (EEOC), Women's Bureau at the Department of Labor (DOL), the Bureau of Labor Statistics (BLS) as well as organizations that track specific industries: Magazine Publishers Association (MPA), Association of the Society of Newspaper Editors (ASNE), Adage (Advertising), Public Relations Society of America (PRSA), Hollywood Reporter (each December) (tracks film industry). Therefore, while various articles mention executive level differential in the newsroom, publishing and broadcast careers, in both private and government reports since 1991 especially, in order to see the differences, we had to put data together (see Table 2.3) from the Bureau of Labor Statistics. We found that 47 percent of those employed in these occupations are women.

The U.S. Labor Department's annual report, Women in the Labor force: A Databook, May 2005, indicates that within the "information industry" (media, telecommunications and entertainment) as a whole, (3.5 million employed), 43.3 percent are women, but their data include libraries and archives (206,000 people); internet service providers (81,000); data processing, hosting and related services (79,000); and wired telecommunication carriers (923,000).[12] What exactly they do in these occupations would be more telling.

In order to compare what so far we had found about occupational differences, we also looked at the EEOC[13] report and chose those categories of occupations we felt closely resembled communication/mass communication fields (acknowledging here that of course all areas involve communication). Based on 2002 data, white men and white women workers outnumbered minorities in all fields (Table 2.4), and women (white and minority) outnumbered workers in periodicals (magazines and journals), books (publishing), radio and TV, miscellaneous publishing and advertising; the ratio is two to one, but in public relations the difference is less than 20 percent.

If we average all percentages of women working as (1) officials & managers and (2) professionals in the above areas of employment, according to the EEOC data, it is 20 percent; that average for men is 24 percent. Minority women average for these occupations only 3.25 percent, so the glass ceiling seems to *gleam* quite clearly for them. Women (white and minority together) outnumber men as officials & managers (one category) and as professionals (another category) in two fields: periodicals and radio & TV broadcast. In all other fields men lead by nine percent on average. Yet, could we claim support for a glass ceiling for all women based on these findings without further study? Our findings so far mean that the rest of the men and women work as technicians, sales workers, office and clerical workers, craft workers, operatives, laborers and service workers.

Again, support for a glass ceiling is somewhat diminished if we review data in Table 2.4 that average 20 percent women—24 percent men in upper levels in these fields because the difference does not seem that significant. It appears that there is more disparity (a glass ceiling) for minority women than for white women, so we decided to go further and look at each mass medium from the top down.

The 2003 EEOC report concludes that little evidence of advancement of women in top communications companies has been found. The percentage of women in executive positions and on boards of directors appears to be stagnant at about 15 percent and 12 percent, respectively. Moreover, the report suggests that there appears to be a second glass ceiling in place.[14] At the same time, the Annenberg Public Policy Center (APPC), Dec. 22, 2003, reported that on average women held 15 percent of executive leadership positions in telecommunications, publishing and printing, entertainment and advertising. However, the APPC report includes companies like SBC Communications (owns AT&T and is known for its broadband and wire solutions); Belo Corporation (owns about 20 TV stations, some newspapers and a business press); R.R. Donnelley & Sons (deals in business print systems, market research, direct marketing campaigns, photography, and more); Charter Communications (in the business of digital cable, high-definition TV, high-speed internet and telephone features like voicemail, caller ID, etc.); and WilTel Communications (purchased in 2005 by Level 3 Communications, an international telecommunications solutions company that counts among its customers U.S. internet service providers and U.S. cable companies. The APPC report does not take into account occupations such as the EEOC reported in the same year.

For our purposes in this text, however with respect to the EEOC report, we wanted to know which other field was the most populated one for both women and men workers (Table 2.4). We were not surprised to find that 15 to 20 percent of all women workers were office and clerical workers; we were surprised to see women outnumber men in periodicals, books, miscellaneous publishing and advertising . Interestingly, we were surprised to find that in radio and TV broadcasting, again they outnumber men as officials and managers and professionals (Table 2.4). It is only in radio & TV broadcasting and miscellaneous publishing that women clerical and office workers outnumber women listed as officials and managers and professionals. Of note, in motion picture production and services, 11 percent of women are office and clerical workers (Table 2.4) but 19 percent of women are officials and mangers and professionals (Table 2.4). What of the still higher executive levels?

*Fortune Magazine*, April 14, 2003, reported there were eight female CEOs in the Fortune 500 companies and another nine in the Fortune 501-1000 companies. An online journal of *The Wall Street Journal,* [the publisher is female, Karen Elliott House; her appointment was criticized for favoritism given her by her husband, Peter R. Kann, CEO and Chairman of Dow Jones & Co. that owns TWSJ] called *CareerJournal.com,* reported findings from a study completed by Catalyst in 2002 that 7.9 percent of positions at the level of executive vice president or higher in all Fortune 500 companies were held by women.[15] More recently, News Corp., owned by Rupert Murdoch (Fox) entered into an agreement with the major stockholders, the Bankcroft family, of Dow Jones, publisher of The Wall Street Journal. News Corp. is discussed later in Table 2.1 with regard to its corporate executives. Dow Jones will probably continue to publish The Wall Street Journal, so we decided to look also at its corporate structure. It lists 15 on its Board of Directors; one is a woman. On its executive management list, there are nine officers and senior management names, two of which are women. It also has a local media group, a consumer media group and an enterprise media group. Altogether the names listed number 21, two of which are female. Its highest-ranking woman is Clare Hart, Executive Vice President, Dow Jones & Company and President of the Dow Jones Enterprise Media Group. [16]

We return to the Annenberg Public Policy Center at the University of Pennsylvania and its 2003 policy center report. The key findings were that women in executive leadership positions of Fortune 500 communications companies (telecommunications, printing and publishing, entertainment and advertising), numbered only 15 percent, but this did not mean they had a position with a "clout title," e.g., the person has significant employer power. Findings in 2003 included the fact that only 208 executive women (or 33 percent) out of a total of 1,247 executives had clout titles. While women comprised 12 percent as board members, no one board had a majority of women, and ten companies or 18 percent of the companies had no women on their boards at all.

In the entertainment and publishing industries, a few of the companies (4 out of 26 publishing and entertainment companies that had more than 20 percent women on their boards), are shown here as examples (Table 2.5).

In the EEOC's March 2004 report, "Glass Ceilings: The Status of Women as Officials and Managers in the Private Sector," only one mass media industry is mentioned and it lumps together newspaper, periodical, book and database publishers. It discloses that in this category there were 39.5 percent women as headquarter managers and 38.18 percent as field managers. Broadcast is lumped in with cable television and internet service providers under the heading of telecommunications and depicts 39.47 percent women as headquarter managers and 42.09 percent women as field managers.

We began this inquiry by looking at the top media conglomerates and at women in top positions in these companies. Clearly, women are making progress. It is true that equally they are not yet the CEOs in the very top rung of the ladder (again, in parent companies), but, below, women in media careers, especially in entertainment (film and television) with magazine publishing running a third, they are in power.

We conclude then that women in media careers are advancing, especially in broadcasting, producing, reporting and editing. Women are etching out career tracks decidedly marked. One question that becomes obvious is why are women not represented in corporate governance and boardrooms?

*The Economist* published a special report about women in business in its July 21, 2005 print edition that asked the same question: Why are women so persistently absent from top corporate jobs? The gist of the article is that the reasons vary from not having enough women on track to become upper-management to women withdrawing to care for family members to women not being able to be part of the old boy's club and able to wine and dine clients quite the same way men have been doing so for years. In an article in *Advertising Age* published in the July 25, 2005 issue, women in power subjected themselves to questioning from a moderator. On stage at the Four Seasons Hotel in New York were Stock Exchange President-Chief Operating Officer Catherine Kinney; IBM General Manager-Healthcare and Life Sciences Dr. Caroline A. Kovac; Ogilvy & Mathern Chairman-CEO Shelly Lazarous; and author and former editor of Harvard Business Review Suzy Welch. Those in attendance included Oxygen Media CEO Geraldine Laybourne. Challenges they discussed included being a woman in the work place and facing things like maternity leave, glass ceilings and comfortable pairs of heels.[17] What these women meant was that women's challenges in the work place are different than men's. Often, women have upper-level careers and still maintain caring for a home, husband and children.

## Offering a Theoretical Explanation

The previously cited literature about the glass ceiling and various commissions formed to explore/examine the impediments in careers for women all review the impediment itself (e.g., the corporate structure, wage disparity, ethnic and gender ratio) and hence the failure of women to advance. True, these commissions do not blame women [we do not blame victims], but neither did they explore instead the women who succeeded despite of or in spite of the obvious placement of a glass ceiling. Sandra Harding's (2002) philosophy about the purpose of research is this: "[It] should not be to construct grand generalizations, but to work closely with people and enhance their understanding and ability to control their own reality. We must engage in the intellectual and political struggle necessary to see social life from the point of view of that which is subjugated instead of from the perspective of the ruling order."[18]

Data then can indicate failures and successes, but examination of those women who succeed can give us answers as to why all women do not. The arguments about women not being able to manage or not being able to maintain heavy workloads or not being able to mature well [i.e., menopause gets in the way] are tired and old. Women do succeed and are slowly penetrating corporate media. Slowly, however, is the operative word. Here is where a theoretical connection can be made about the progress.

Social Identity Theory was developed by H. Tajfel and J. C. Turner (1986) when they published work about inter-group behavior and its connection to identity and image of the company. The theory identifies a person with several selves that correspond to groups of membership to which a person belongs. Group membership then creates in-group/self categorization and enhancement in ways that favor the in-group at the expense of the out-group. Hence, we assign people to categories based on color, ethnicity, religion, etc. Also, we identify with groups that we perceive ourselves to belong to. So categorization and identification are two of the central ideas of the theory.[19]

Another theory, the third, is social comparison (developed by Festinger, 1954[20]). In order to evaluate ourselves, we compare ourselves with similar others. We belong to groups where we can find some kind of prestige, important for self-concepts. In corporate group structures the higher executive levels are small groups of people that perceive themselves to be high in status (which they are in terms of power and money) and have already chosen dimensions for themselves. Changes, if they are to happen, upset the dimensions and identity conflict ensues.

So identity of an organization is what makes the organizational life possible. Balmer and Soenen (1999) took the corporate (or organizational) identity metaphor further in a study of 20 corporations in the UK and found that the way in which members identified with the organization visually was the primary vehicle to affect a change in the organization's identity. They found, for the most part, that companies were vision driven together strategic vision as the operative words.[21]

Identity conflict occurs when changes occur, such as a merger. Conflict is diminished if the organizational members perceive a sense of continuity of identity. If not, the organization faces calamity (van Knippenberg et al, 2002).

Rather than perceiving change as positive, change in the status quo—the CEO, the Board, the Corporate Governance—literally shakes up an organization. No wonder, then, that change in media corporations at the very top levels are occurring slowly. When Sumner Redstone (CBS) steps out of the picture, will his daughter, Sharon Redstone, the current COO step into the picture? By the time this text is published, we should know the answer.

Often, an heir succeeds the father to keep the organization stable. Katherine Graham succeeded her husband as CEO of the Washington Post; her son, Donald Graham has stepped in. Liz Mohn (mentioned earlier) was up for succession of her husband, Reinhold Mohn, as CEO of Bertelsmann AG but as stated earlier was replaced by Gunter Thielen instead. The key to change is the creative ability of the corporate in-group to visualize a new identity. A group member that does not "look like them" or "act like them" or "think like them" has a difficult time getting accepted.

The foregoing discussion about a theoretical underpinning to women continuing to be "under" a glass ceiling is in no way meant to be an excuse for the glass ceiling. Each day we see women names pop up in media—Sara Polley directed a movie nominated for an Oscar, "Darling," starring Julie Christie, and Cathleen Black, president of Hearst Magazines, published a book in 2007 called *Basic Black*, about her four decades in a media career. Our argument is that slowly and surely women who bring in the bottom-line for both print and entertainment media will create an identity for themselves, are creating an in-group identity already, that other group members will want to be part of, regardless of looks, actions or philosophies. We further believe that women will continue to nibble away at the glass [or jello] ceiling. It takes time, but time has always been a factor for women and careers.

## Summary

With regard to mass media careers, there are not many women in "clout positions,"—presidents and CEOs of all the major media companies, so we could argue that factual findings support the glass ceiling conceptual structure clearly in place. However, we have found in our research that women are continuing to climb regardless of the glass ceiling, and women especially in the broadcast and film industries are obtaining more and more clout positions.

The next chapter begins a discussion of the book publishing industry.

*Table 2.1 The Top News/Entertainment Conglomerates*

| Company | Owns | CEO | Male corporate executives | Female corporate executives | Men on Board of Directors | Women on Board of Directors |
|---|---|---|---|---|---|---|
| News Corp. | Fox Broadcasting Cable, Film, Television Stations, Publishing Companies | Rupert Murdoch | 11 | 1 | 13 | -0- |
| GE | 80% of NBC Universal and numerous NBC stations | Jeffrey R.Immelt | 21 | 5 | 9 | 2 |
| Viacom | CBS Stations, Cable Channels and Radio Stations and Paramount Pictures besides Simon & Schuster and Blockbuster | Sumner Redstone, Exec. Chairman of the Board of Viacom and Chairman of the Board of CBS Corporation; Tom Freston is President and CE of Viacom and CBS | 10 (Viacom) | 5 | 10 | 2 |
| TimeWarner | Books, Magazines, Turner Broadcasting, Cable and Film and TV Distribution | Richard D. Parsons | 7 | 2 | 9 | 2 |

(continued)

*Table 2.1 The Top News/Entertainment Conglomerates (continued)*

| Company | Owns | CEO | Male corporate executives | Female corporate executives | Men on Board of Directors | Women on Board of Directors |
|---|---|---|---|---|---|---|
| Disney | Film, publishing, musc, multimedia, broadcast and cable stations | Robert A. Iger | 10 | 2 | 12 | 2 |
| Sony Pictures | Sony Pictures Entertainment, Columbia TriStar Motion Picture Group, Sony Pictures Home Entertainment, Sony Pictures Television Group, Sony Pictures consumer Products, Sony Pictures Digital, Sony Pictures Studios, Game Show Network, Movielink | Howard Stringer (Also Vice Chair Sony Corporation) | SPE only: 3 | 1 | Sony Corporation: 12 | 1 |

*(continued)*

*Table 2.1 The Top News/Entertainment Conglomerates (continued)*

| Company | Owns | CEO | Male corporate executives | Female corporate executives | Men on Board of Directors | Women on Board of Directors |
|---------|------|-----|--------------------------|----------------------------|--------------------------|----------------------------|
| Bertelsmann | European television, U.S. division, altogether company owns radio, BMG Music Group, Random House, internatioal book and music clubs | Gunter Thielsen | Executive Board has 7 men; 0 women; also 26 male and 2 female executives listed in company's corporate center | 2 | 14 | 1 |
| TOTALS | | | 105 | 17 | 76 | 10 |

Compiled by viewing www.cjr.org/tools/owners as well as corporate web pages.

### Table 2.2. The Wage Gap, by Gender and Race

| Year | White Men | Black Men | Hispanic Men | White Women | Black Women | Hispanic Women |
|------|-----------|-----------|--------------|-------------|-------------|----------------|
| 2003 | 100% | 78.2% | 63.3% | 75.6% | 65.4% | 54.3% |

(In other words, in 2003 white women were earning 75.6 cents per $1.00 that men were earning; Black women were earning 65.4 cents and Hispanic women, 54.3 cents). (Source: National Committee on Pay Equity (Information Please Database, 2005 Pearson Education, Inc.)

### Table 2.3. U.S. Female Labor Force Working in Mass Media Related Jobs 2004

| Occupation | Total Employed | Percent | Women |
|------------|----------------|---------|-------|
| Producers and Directors | 137,000 | 32.3 | 44,251 |
| Announcers | 54,000 | 21.6 | 11,664 |
| News Analysts, reporters and correspondents | 81,000 | 53.7 | 43,497 |
| Editors | 164,000 | 53.9 | 88,396 |
| Writers and Authors | 194,000 | 55.1 | 106,894 |
| Broadcast and sound engineering technicians and radio operators | 92,000 | 12.1 | 11,132 |
| Public Relations Specialists | 133,000 | 61.1 | 81,263 |
| Miscellaneous media and communication workers | 74,000 | 70.0 | 51,800 |
| Advertising | 70,000 | 60.3 | 42,210 |
| Female Actors | | | |
| **TOTAL EMPLOYED AND AVERAGE PERCENT** | **999,000** | **46.67** | **466,233** |

Compiled from data in Bureau of Labor Statistics (www.bls.gov)

## Table 2.4. EEOC Aggregate Reports at 2002

| Unit | Motion Pictures Production & Services | Newspapers | Periodicals | Books | Radio & TV Broadcasting | Misc. Publishing | Advertising | Public Relations & Mgmt. |
|---|---|---|---|---|---|---|---|---|
| Total Employment | 42,436 | 298,448 | 64,796 | 75,697 | 130,920 | 60,256 | 102,693 | 481,257 |
| Men | 24,543 | 168,654 | 29,042 | 35,201 | 77,399 | 28,541 | 39,537 | 262.826 |
| Women | 17,893 | 129,794 | 35,754 | 40,496 | 53,521 | 31,715 | 63,156 | 218,431 |
| Total percent all women as officials and managers and professionals | 19% | 19% | 26% | 10% | 28% | 21% | 18% | 22% |
| Total percent of all men as officials and managers and professionals | 27% | 21% | 22% | 15% | 20% | 36% | 21% | 33% |
| Other field where majority women worked in each genre | Office & Clerical Workers | Office & Clerical Workers | Office & Clerical Workers | Office & Clerical Workers | Office & Clerical Workers | Office & Clerical Workers | Office & Clerical Workers | Office & Clerical Workers |
| Percent of all workers | 11% | 12% | 18% | 14% | 18% | 16% | 14% | 14% |

Table 2.4. EEOC Aggregate Reports at 2002 (continued)

| Unit | Motion Pictures Production & Services | Newspapers | Periodicals | Books | Radio & TV Broadcasting | Misc. Publishing | Advertising | Public Relations & Mgmt. |
|---|---|---|---|---|---|---|---|---|
| Other field where majority women worked in each genre | Technicians | Operatives | Sales | Craft Workers | Technicians | Sales | Sales | Technicians |
| Percent of all workers | 6% | 10% | 5% | 9% | 17% | 7% | 6% | 5% |

EEOC Aggregate Reports Nos. SIC 781, 271, 272, 273, 48731, 874 in order.[22]

*Table 2.5. Women as Members of Boards of Directors 2003*

| Company | Total People on Board/ Directors | Total Women on Board/ Directors | Total Executives | Total Female Executives |
|---|---|---|---|---|
| Gannett (publishing) | 8 | 2  (25%) | 32 | 8  (25%) |
| NY Times (publishing) | 13 | 4  (31%) | 21 | 6  (29%) |
| Scholastic (publishing) | 15 | 4  (27%) | 16 | 8  (50%) |
| Walt Disney (entertainent) | 17 | 4  (24%) | 24 | 3  (13%) |

Annenberg Public Policy Center Report, December 2003.

# Notes

1. http://money.cnn.com/magazines/fortune/mostpowerfulwomen/2005/perennials/index.html.

2. Sellers, P. The Women of Viacom. Fortune, October 11, 2006; http://money.conn.com/magazines/fortune/fortune_archive/2006/10/16/8388650/index.htm.

3. Northwestern study.

4. Media Report to Women's web page is www.mediareporttowomen.com/statistics.htm.

5. Falk, Erika, Washington Research director and Erin Grizard, Research Assistant in "The Glass Ceiling Persists: The 3rd Annual APPC Report on Women Leaders in Communication companies," published by the Annenberg Public Policy Center of the University of Pennsylvania, December 2003; p. 6.

6. Quoted in Wrigley, Brenda J. "Glass Ceiling? What Glass Ceiling? A Qualitative Study of How Women View the Glass Ceiling in Public Relations and Communications Management." *Journal of Public Relations Research*, 14(1) (2002): 27-55.

7. Tomaskovic-Devey, Donald. Race, ethnic, and gender earnings inequality, the sources and consequences of employment segregation. A Report to the Glass Ceiling Commission, U.S. Department of Labor, January (1994): 2.

8. Clara Jeffrey, editorial, Limited Ambitions. January/February (2006); www.motherjones.com/news/exhibit/2006/01/limited_ambitions.html.

9. See www.womenenews.org.

10. See www.catalyst.org.

11. Find them at www.cyberwerks.com/dataline/.

12. This includes newspaper publishers, publishing, except newspapers and software, motion pictures and video industries, radio and television broadcasting and cable, wire telecommunications carriers, internet service providers, data processing, hosting and related services and libraries and archives (1992).

13. All EEOC reports are from BLS web pages, www.eeoc.gov.

14. EEOC Report. . .

15. Women Corporate Officers and Top Earners, 2002 Catalyst Census of Women Corporate Officers and Top Earners. www.catalyst.org/knowledge/titles/title.php?page=cen_WOTE02.

16. Go to www.dowjones.com/TheCompany/ExecutiveManagement/ExecutiveManagement.htm.

17. Footnote the Economist issue here.

18. Piatelli, D. and D. Leckenby (2002). "Sandra Harding." This is a profile piece about Harding's guest lectures Feb. 25-27, 2002 at Boston College. Go to www.bc.edu/schools/cas/sociology/vss/harding.

19.  Tajfel, H. and J.C. Turner (1986). The social identity theory of inter-group behavior. In S. Worche and L.W. Austin (eds.), *Psychology of Intergroup Relations*. Chicago: Nelson-Hall.

20.  Festinger, L. (1954). A theory of social comparison processes. *Human Relations*, 7, p. 117-140.

21.  Balmer, J.M.T. and G.B. Soenen (1999). The acid test of corporate identity management. *Journal of Marketing Management*, 15, 69-92; 74-74.

22.  Go to www.eeoc.gov/stats/jobpat/2002/sic3 and put in search link for the report number.

# Chapter Three

# Nothing Like a Good Book

Book sales totaled $24.2 Billion in 2006. Adult paperback books sales account for $2.3 billion; children and young adult books fell slightly; audio books fell also; E-books saw a 24% increase; mass market paperbacks grew as well as higher education sales.[1]

> FYI—Neither Carole nor Lee has ever worked in the book publishing world; however, they have worked in the textbook field as reviewers and editors. They certainly have learned much about the field in developing and writing this text.

Book publishing began with Gutenberg's movable press and the duplication of the Bible in his printing house in eastern Germany, in the town of Mintz, in 1456.[2] The invention was named the number-one innovation for the last millennium in a poll for on-line readers of the BBC News, January 2000.[3] Being able to replicate text material changed everything. Once people became more literate, they wanted more information. Novels in the latter part of the eighteenth century and throughout the nineteenth century stimulated people in terms of relationships, children, hardships, quests, wars, and travel. The more literate one became, the more successful one wanted to become. While it is obvious we are living in a technological age, and we may indeed live in a wireless world by 2020, one can then only wonder if the paper book will still be around. The Kindle is a hand-held electronic book sold by Amazon.com and can download books, magazines and newspapers; it weighs only 10 ounces!

In the middle of downloading a J.K. Rowling (Harry Potter author) or her successor, will a video-message appear before us, from a friend perhaps anxious to talk to us? Even if such a futuristic vision becomes a reality, the prediction we, the authors, make is that there will always be a desire to read a good book, in one form or another.

This chapter pertains to book publishing, editing and authoring books. In the magazine, newspaper and internet chapters, we will again touch upon publishing and editing careers for women. We look first at major book publishing companies.

# Major Book Publishers

According to the *Vault Career Guide to Book Publishing*, in 2002, there were 85,000 employees at book publishing companies with two billion books sold in the U.S. every year, 60,000 of which are new titles. The largest book publishing employers are divided into three areas: trade books (Random House, The Penguin Group, HarperCollins, Simon & Schuster, Time Warner Books [may be sold to Lagardere, owner of Hachette Filipacchi Medias], FSG/St.Martin's/Macmillan); educational/ professional books (Thomson Corporation, Reed Elsevier, McGraw-Hill, Pearson Education, Walter Klicwer, Houghton Mifflin, John Wiley & Sons); and children's books (Scholastic).[4]

Of the 14 listed above, only six parent companies are located in the United States. As Vault points out, each of these companies has many divisions and within each division are a number of imprints or lines, such as Random House's imprints (lines): Bantam, Doubleday, Dell, Pantheon, Knopf, Ballantine, Fodor's.[5]

Book publishing categories include fiction, nonfiction, educational and professional. Fiction and nonfiction are considered trade books because these books are sold to people in the trade (booksellers and wholesalers). Individuals purchase books from booksellers (e.g.,Books-a-Million, Barnes & Noble), and trade books comprise 32% of all book sales. Educational titles are sold to educators and educational institutions, and professional titles are sold to professional organizations like hospitals, law schools, research institutions and accounting practices. The trade book categories of fiction and nonfiction include children/juvenile fiction and nonfiction (ages 0-18).

Educational publishing represents 31% of total book sales and is split evenly between elementary-high school (ElHi) and college (HigherEd) textbooks. The growth of online used book companies that offer textbooks for sale bites into profits but educational publishing continues to be profitable.

Professional publishing represents 19% of total book sales and books are usually in the scientific, technical and medical matters (STM).

The rest of the publishing market (17%) is divided among smaller niches: religious, general reference (dictionaries, for example), series (Time-Life books, for example), and specific academic and miscellaneous books from smaller presses.[6]

## Who Owns the Book Publishing Companies?

Among the top 18 publishing companies, McGraw-Hill, Scholastic and Reader's Digest Association are the only book publishers. (See Table 3.1 appended). R.R. Donnelly is listed as number 275 in the 500 rank in Fortune, but they qualify more as printers than publishers. If the company does layout and editorial guidance, and if one can send materials directly to them for publication, then the company would qualify as a publisher. According to their web page, R. R. Donnelly does book publishing from the technical side and in magazine publishing we suspect again it is the technical rendering that is offered. Scholastic, on the other hand, is a book publishing company that includes original children's books, e.g., *Clifford the Big Red Dog* and the *Harry Potter* series. They rank number 701 in the Fortune 1000 rank of businesses. A company such as Reader's Digest (rank 666) also publishes in the trade magazine area. Gannett (rank 283), Tribune (rank 348), Knight-Ridder (rank 568), Washington Post (rank 526) and the New York Times Company (rank 525), however, are all newspaper-publishing companies.

Today, book publishing is a $25 billion dollar industry according to the U.S. Dept. of Labor's Industrial Outlook of 2006, which means it is not all that big. Vault points out that Microsoft, alone, is a $32 billion revenue company by comparison, and it is interesting because sales continue to climb in the adult trade book category even though the internet offers books on-line. Newspapers, however, by year's end 2001 were not doing well with net revenue, down for Tribune Co., Knight Ridder (that subsequently sold all its newspapers) and The New York Times, to name a few.[7] Table 3.1 outlines publishing companies that fall under the Fortune 500 umbrella.

# Careers in Book Publishing

In the 2006 Publishers Weekly salary survey, the average income for men in publishing was $99,442 and $63,747 for women. Publishers Weekly claims that the disparity is because there are many more women on the editorial side (74%) of thep. business, while mean dominate (60%) on the management side.[8]

In management earnings in all industries, the Bureau of Labor Statistics reported median hourly earnings of $54.72 in 2002. In book publishing, these salary positions can be found as well as those of writers and editors. In these fields, again, the BLS reported for 2002 that median annual earnings for writers and authors were $42,790 with the lowest 10 percent earning less than $21,320 and the highest earning $85,140. Salaried editors' median annual earnings were $41,170 in 2002 with the lowest less than $24,010 and the highest more than $76,620. Technical writers, another career field within corporate publishing, in 2002 had a median annual earning of $50,580 with the lowest less than $30,270 and the highest more than $80,900.

The position of CEO in book publishing commands, probably, larger paychecks based on experience in book publishing and previous profit-making. Women usually work as editors, copy editors and in marketing and advertising departments of publishing houses as well as in management, but more and more women are getting into the top positions (discussed further down). A 1999 survey of women and minorities conducted by the Association of American Publishers received responses from six publishers [names not shared] who disclosed that 28.9 percent in executive and senior managements were women; whereas, in editorial and sales, percentages were 55 and 70 respectively.[9] The companies preferred to remain anonymous, so AAP could not divulge their names. The organization of a book publisher varies according to size. The company, if a large one, will have a president of a category in publishing (e.g., president of professional/grade markets; science/technical medical markets; higher ed; Eli-Hi markets) as well as an international or European President. Each of these people is also a vice president and each reports to the President and CEO.

Within the company, the president of professional/trade titles will have imprints or divisions who report to him/her. One division of Random House is Doubleday. That imprint has a department called "publishing" and five arms of publishing report to the head of the division's publishing that include marketing, editorial, sales, rights and production. Under "editorial" careers, there is editor, copyeditor, proofreader and production.

- **Editor**—broken down into acquisition editor, senior editor and editors-in-chief (defined below)
- **Copy editor**—edits text for jacket covers of books as well as advertisement description of the book
- **Proofreader**—checks for grammar, semantics, colloquialisms, and sentence structures
- **Production**—includes layout/graphic design skilled people.

## Best Seller Lists

The next question is will the *New York Times* best-seller list still be around in 2020? Laura J. Miller writes that even though best-seller lists are highly debated as to their value, the lists, such as that of *The New York Times*, continue to maintain a voice of authority. The question debated is whether or not the lists adequately reflect real dollar sales? Miller makes this point:

> [D]espite general agreement in the industry that the lists do not accurately reflect what books are the country's top sellers, major publishers and booksellers have an interest in maintaining the authority of the lists.[10]

The concept of a best-seller list goes back to 1895 when a best-seller list appeared in a magazine called *The Bookman*, which later sold in 1918 and its new owners devised what they called, a Books of the Month list. In 1912, *The Publishers' Weekly,* still publishing today, began its own then best-seller list taking into account the Books of the Month list. *The New York Times* began its list in 1931; it contained five fiction and four nonfiction books. Today, the *Times* surveys about 4,000 bookstores and an unstated number of wholesale book outlets for its data.[11]

In the last 50 years, few female authors have made it as best sellers. Book publishers would argue that this is due to consumer taste. Yet, data reveal a correlation: that female publishers rarely rise to the top in the book publishing world and female best sellers have been rare.

## Online Self-Publishing (*e*Publishing)

The 2006 industry statistics by the Association of American Publishers (AAP) reported that E-books saw a 24.1% increase in 2006 at $54 million, with a compound growth rate of 65% since 2002 while mass market paperbacks saw a growth of only 4.6 percent in 2006.[12] Clearly, online publishing is economically possible for women wage-earners since today these publishing companies charge as little as $300 for an *e*book to appear online for download. Often, at some sites, there is no upfront charge at all. We should see an increase overall in men self-publishing as well over the next few years.

# Women's Careers in Publishing

- **Authors vs. writers**—an author is considered a writer but not all writers are considered authors. A published piece has an author, sometimes unnamed. Writers who place text on an ad or write the words for a commercial are called copy writers, not authors. There are authors of books, nonfiction and fiction, journals, articles, dissertations and theses.
- **Editor**—the editor in book publishing has many hats—maintaining contact with authors and literary agents, negotiating contracts, and handling publishing details—but also is responsible for final line-editing of manuscripts.
- **Acquisitions editors**—might be senior editors or editors who have come from the sales end of publishing; nevertheless, he/she is responsible for identifying growing new markets and acquiring new and promising manuscripts.
- **Editors-in-chief**—will be the head of editorial responsible for overall direction of the division and maintaining quality standards, budget concerns and all other human resource decisions for the editorial department.[13]

In essence, then, authors may put words on paper, but it is the editor who manicures the words.

# Spotlight

Hilary Claggett is the Senior Editor at Potomac Books, Inc. Here is how she got into the business:

*I have been an acquisitions editor for twelve years. Many people come to this profession from other fields, including academia and journalism, but I began my career in publishing as an Editorial Assistant at the Carnegie Council on Ethics and International Affairs. I chose that organization because it was related to my master's degree in international affairs from Columbia University. I soon realized that I enjoyed editing in any subject. I began my acquisitions career in library reference, moving from that to business and economics and then to current events, politics, and international affairs. I am happy to say that my career has come full circle, uniting my academic background and all of my experience in the intervening years. It is challenging but rewarding work.*

## How to Get Started in a Career in the Book Publishing Industry

In this business it is best to start interning at any book publishing company that will take you on. Usually interns are still in college and either seniors or graduate students with majors in either English or journalism. A student will have a good chance of getting accepted as an intern if he or she has editing and writing experience while in college, such as work on the college newspaper. Clearly, to be an editor, one must be a formidable writer who really understands grammar and punctuation. An understanding of the Associated Press style manual is a must as well. For a person to become an editor at a large publishing house, that person must build a sizeable portfolio of work he or she published as well as edited. It is best to get the foot in the door at a small press if a big city is not within reach. Experience is the key to this career.

For jobs in publishing, look at Vault, an industry newsletter, at www.vault.com; search for Publishing Career Path.

While online, instant or print-on-demand publishing may indeed create an "unraveling" of the book publishing industry in the future, the fact is that today publishing a book in traditional venues is tough. One of the most successful mystery writers of the last century, Agatha Christie (1890-1976), were she still alive might currently be able to publish based on the title of her books alone. According to a new computer model that examines book titles versus each book's sales, the titles with short, catchy, figurative or abstract language sell well. The outcome of the study is that titles of books if codified with 11 title attributes, can be scored; the higher the score up to 1.0, the more likely success in sales. Hence, Christie's last novel, published in 1976, just before her death, called *Sleeping Murder*, received a .83 score predicting higher than average sales. Robert Stein, in a *Newsweek* article, dated Jan. 16, 2006, noted that the computer rating doesn't always work, e.g.,*The DaVinci Code* had only a 36 percent chance of finding a wide audience.[14] By March, 2004, there were purportedly 6.8 million copies in print.[15]

A glance at the best sellers lists supports the argument for short, figurative language in the titles: Porter's *Ship of Fools*, Suzanne's *Valley of the Dolls*, and Winson's *Forever Amber*. The 2005 best selling novel, and another catchy title, *Eleven on Top*, is also by a female author, Janet Evanovich. The top five best sellers in hardback fiction the week of July 17, 2005 saw five women novelists top this chart: Besides Evanovich, *The Historian* by Elizabeth Kostova was 2nd place, *Miracle* by Danielle Steel was 4th place and *The Mermaid Chair* by Sue Monk Kidd was 5th place. In 3rd place was Dan Brown, *DaVinci Code*.[16]

Meanwhile, J.K. Rowling's titles are anything but catching for adults but succeed quite a bit with children. Her novel, *Harry Potter and the Chamber of Secrets*, released in 1999 saw her first three novels as well reach #1 position in best sellers in quick succession.[17]

# Women CEOs and Fortune 500 Top Ten List

A review of CEO's of various companies on the Fortune 500 web page (www.fortune.com) reveals in fact that there are only nine Fortune 500 companies that are run by women (chief executive officers). The list includes only one media company, The New York Times Company, publisher of the daily *New York Times,* which will be discussed in the newspaper chapter. However, women are in other various top positions at Scholastic: Mary Winston is Executive V.P. and CFO at Scholastic;

Deborah A. Forte is Executive V.P. and Pres., Scholastic Media; Lisa Holton and Margery W. Mayer are executive vice presidents; Judith A. Newman is Sr. V.P and President, Book Clubs and Scholastic At Home and there are three more women listed on their Executives page.[18] Louise Dennys is executive publisher of Alfred A. Knopf Canada (named after the Knopf publishing company out of New York) and executive vice president of Random House of Canada (distributing house for Random House Books). Susan Petersen Kennedy is President, Penguin Group (USA) (owned by Pearson) which is the second-largest English-language trade book publisher in the world and which publishes under a wide range of imprints, e.g., Dutton, Grosset & Dunlap, New American Library, Riverhead Books, Viking and more. Meanwhile, at Penguin Putnam [owned by Pearson], Phyllis Grann who was chief executive and president left her position in 2001 and obtained a position at Random House as senior editor of Doubleday Broadway Publishing Group. Pearson, also owner of the Penguin Group, lists two women on the Board: Marjorie Scardino, Chief Executive, and Rona Fairhead, Chief Executive, Financial Times Group.[19]

One of the oldest and largest publishing houses today is HarperCollins Publishers that was started in 1817 by brothers James and John Harper and William Collins, out of London. Today, HarperCollins is a global publishing company due largely to Rupert Murdoch's News Corporation's acquisition in 1987 and has revenues that topped $1Billion in 2002 according to its own web page (www.harpercollins.com). Jane Friedman is President and CEO of the company located in New York City, but the reach of the company extends to the United Kingdom, Canada and Australia.

Friedman began working for Random House, another large publishing company, in 1972 as a dictaphone typist in a large typing pool. Today, such an employment concept is obsolete. She worked in every area of publishing and rose through the ranks at Random House to become executive vice president before moving to HarperCollins. She claims that she has not experienced the "glass ceiling" that women say exists. After she accepted a prestigious Matrix Award in 2001 she told a BBC interviewer, "I proved to the world of publishing that there is no glass ceiling."[20]

Not all women get this type of break. It is true, according to the Bureau of Labor Statistics, women held half of all management, professional and related occupations in 2004. However, in the publishing world, that percent was about 1 percent.

# Minority Women in Publishing

Among the best selling books is *Amazing Peace* by Maya Angelou, the only African American on the list. Yet, African American women are plentiful in book publishing. The Census Bureau reported that in 2000 there were in fact, almost 4,000 included in the census as writers and authors (a total of 106,700 were women); Asian included about 2,000 and Hispanic or Latino included about 2,700 women in this category.

The most popular or better-known minority female writers today include Toni Cade Bambara (*Medley* (1977); Maxine Hong Kingston (*Tripmaster Monkey: His Fake Book* (1989); Toni Morrison (*Beloved*, 1987)); Alice Walker (*Everyday Use* (1973), *The Color Purple* (1982); Sandra Cisneros (*The House on Mango Street* (1984), *Women Hollering Creek* (1991) ); Judy Ortiz Cofer (*The Latin Deli* [1993]; and Diane Glancy (*Firesticks* [1993]).[21]

Toni Morrison was awarded the Pulitzer Price in 1988 and the Nobel Peace Prize in 1993. Her works include *Beloved, Sula* and others. Alice Walker is best known for her novel, *The Color Purple,* published in 1982 and made into a movie starring Whoopi Goldberg and Oprah Winfrey in 1986.

Clearly, these women authors are a minority. The 55,000 women writers/authors (and presumably this would include writers who don't publish necessarily in their jobs), listed in 2004 by the Bureau of Labor Statistics included: 3.6% African American, 2.2% Asian and 2.6% Hispanic. In the 2002 Equal Employment Opportunity Commission (EEOC) report under the category of books, there are more Black[22] women employed in this industry than Black men and other minorities; however, under total employment, Whites are the vast majority: 35,201 Men and 40,496 Women; 2,316 Black Men and 3,341 Black Women (one-third work as Office and Clerical Workers, 222 are listed as Officials and Managers and 434 are under the heading of Professionals).

About publishing, in 2003, the following employee comment was posted with regard to working at McGraw-Hill:

> Within the educational publishing group, it [McGraw-Hill] is very much an "old boys' network" . . . Gender discrimination runs rampant— unless you are part of the club. The sales force is approximately 60%

women, 40% men; at the middle management and upper management level, it's a dramatic flip flop . . . many, many more men than women . . . very little diversity . . . a lily-white company.[23]

# Publishing and the Glass Ceiling

In 1997, Gayle Feldman wrote about women in the publishing industry. Her article, Breaking Through the Glass Ceiling, was published in *Publishers Weekly*, a trade magazine for the industry. She reported then that typically, women were not CEOs in the publishing business. Rather, she wrote, women had "infiltrated the inner sanctum sufficiently to have made the titles of publisher and president and editor-in-chief their own." While women were corporate counsel (attorneys) for some of the biggest publishing conglomerates, they held jobs as sales reps and sales directors on the inside. They might be vice presidents in charge of marketing, publicity, advertising and in educational publishing even CFOs (Chief Financial Officers). But women, like Phyllis Grann, CEO of Penguin Putnam was atypical, then.

Interestingly, Feldman reported then statistics about people who work in book publishing are lacking. The 1996 Labor Statistics disclosed that 1.4 million workers were employed in printing, publishing and allied industries (that included magazines) and that more than 41 percent were female. More recent 2006 data indicate in publishing except newspapers and software 324,000 are employed with 57 percent women.

Currently, the low number of female CEOs among the Fortune 500 companies seems to indicate that although women still have a hard time climbing the corporate ladder, some, such as Jane Friedman and others mentioned earlier, do climb the ladder in publishing in top level management positions. Since the 1999 demographic survey of publishers conducted by the Association of American Publishers, reported that in six major publishing houses, 70.9 percent of editorial staff were women, 78.2 percent of entry management were women but only 28.9 percent of executive senior management were women.[24] Things are changing. The researchers and authors of this text have been tracking women in media positions for four years now and within just a couple of months management teams will change with the inclusion of another woman. When one looks at the top 12 largest publishing companies with 232 executives, 52 (22 percent) are women with Scholastic Publishing Company and at the New York Times Publishing Company seven out of 19 (37 percent) are women.[25] One publishing company on this list, Gannett, shows Susan

Clark-Johnson as Chairman and CEO, Senior Group President of the Phoenix Newspapers Inc. and Gannett Pacific Newspaper group, which we discuss in more detail in the next chapter about newspapers.

What is interesting to learn is that out of 194,000 people listed in 2004 as holding positions of writers and authors, 55.1 percent are women; 3.6 percent are Black (African-American) women; 2.2 percent are Asian women; and 2.6 percent are Hispanic women.

Women nevertheless succeed despite all odds. Our diversified diva for this chapter is Dr. Joyce Brothers who early on learned how to diversify her talents.

## Diversified Diva: Dr. Joyce Brothers

If we think of divas as brands, Dr. Joyce Brothers [and we never hear her referred to as Joyce Brothers without the title] would pop up as a brand name associated with analysis, self-help, logic, reason and celebrity. Joyce Brothers is not our typical media *diva*, but she is a diva nevertheless. We place her here in the book chapter because of the dozens of books she has authored and the fact that her work is published in 26 languages. Like a diversified diva does, she has crossed easily into other media genres. She has made 25 appearances in movies, about half of which as herself; she regularly broadcasts on the NBC Radio Network—Mondays through Fridays; she is a frequent guest on network television programs including NBC-TV's Tonight Show, Conan O'Brien, previously on *Jag,* and various panel shows; her book titles range from *How to Get Whatever You Want* to *Widowed.* She is a noted psychologist, columnist (writing a daily column that is published in more than 350 newspapers), and a business consultant, besides being a wife and mother. She may not have opted for celebrity status in the media, but clearly most people have heard of Dr. Joyce Brothers.

She was born in 1928 as Joyce Diane Bauer in New York City. Her public fame perhaps began when she became a two-time winner of television's, *The $64,000 Question* produced with great success in the 1950s until the scandal of quiz show fraud. The scandal was the subject of a motion picture, *The Quiz Show,* (1999) starring Ralph Finnes as Charles Van Doren.

Brothers is a graduate of Cornell University and received her Ph.D. from Columbia University. She was married to Dr. Milton Brothers, an internist for 39 years; he died in 1989 of cancer. Together they raised a daughter, Lisa. Brothers resides in New York City and is in much demand as a consultant and speaker. Occasionally, we still spot her in films in cameo roles; she offers no self-concern about her movie career and gives one the impression no matter the role, even on radio, that she is pretty even-keeled.

A United Press International poll named her as one of the 10 Most Influential American Women; the Greenwich College Research Center listed her among the 10 women Most Admired by College Students; and in another poll, conducted by Good Housekeeping magazine, she was placed in a 10th place tie with Golda Meir of Israel as the Most Admired Women in the World.

Dr. Joyce Brothers exemplifies how a woman can break glass ceilings. She, like other divas that we mention in this text, is a smart business woman; hence, long ago she figured out that public appearances would generate more revenue as an author and more books would generate more public appearances.[26]

# Summary

The glass ceiling may well be unbreakable for minorities as they try to climb corporate ladders in book publishing. Since we have so few women in executive positions in mass media venues, it is not surprising that there are also fewer in book publishing. While it appears that companies like Scholastic have a high number of females working within the company, still on the management, executive level, other publishing companies fall short of gender diversity. Whether this is an anomaly only in the publishing industry when comparing other mass media industries, the remaining chapters will disclose.

In this chapter, what you learned was that book publishing is divided up into categories (trade, educational and professional), that of the top 14 companies, each with a CEO, chief executive officer, and only six are U.S. parent companies, and that these companies all have imprints or divisions where there are also presidents. To repeat, according to Labor Statistics for 2006, there were 324,000 people employed in publishing (that did not include newspapers and software), and 57 percent were women.[27]

While more and more women writers are producing best sellers—Elizabeth Kostova, author of *The Historian*, about the mythical figure of Dracula, was still on the best seller list in the summer of 2005. Publishing house, Little Brown, believed in the novel so much that Kostova received a $2 million advance.[28] Still, the fact is that the best selling novels over the last four decades have been written by men. Some would argue that choices in publishing are made at the executive level based on the gender of the executives. While there are not women in the book publishing industry at the CEO level except for Jane Friedman mentioned earlier, the EEOC report of 2002 indicates that women outnumber men under the heading of Professionals and come close to a balance under Officials and Managers.

Book publishing then remains a media venue where the glass ceiling is firmly in place for women executives and authors, and it may be only with luck and much perseverance that a woman could climb to the CEO level in the industry. Women, however, who diversify themselves as brand names after reaching success and have vast recognition of their names have no glass ceiling to contend with, not the *diversified diva,* like Dr. Joyce Brothers.

In the next chapter, we will discuss the newspaper publishing industry and women's careers.

**Table 3.1 Book Publishers in Fortune 500 Ranking**

| Company | 500 Rank | Revenue in $millions |
|---|---|---|
| R.R. Donnelley & Sons | 275 | 7,791 |
| Gannett | 283 | 7,381 |
| Tribune | 348 | 5,726 |
| McGraw-Hill | 375 | 5,254 |
| New York Times | 5,254 | 3,304 |
| Washington Post | 526 | 3,300 |
| Knight-Ridder | 567 | 3,014 |
| Reader's Digest Assn. | 666 | 2,389 |
| Scholastic | 701 | 2,234 |
| E.W. Scripps | 720 | 2,168 |
| American Greetings | 755 | 2,009 |
| Cenveo | 837 | 1,743 |
| Dow Jones | 862 | 1,672 |
| Dex Media | 887 | 1,602 |
| Deluxe | 890 | 1,596 |
| Banta | 911 | 1,523 |
| Belo | 918 | 1,510 |
| Primedia | 982 | 1,359 |

From: www.Fortune.com (2005 Fortune 500 List)

# Notes

1. See http://publishers.org/main/industryStats/indStats_02.htm.
2. WWW.Guttenberg.net is a nonprofit database free to internet users.
3. BBC News, January, 2000 reported that Johannes Gutenberg, inventory of the printing press was voted the top inventors by online readers (news.bbc.co.uk).
4. Manning, Matt and the staff of Vault (2004). *Vault Career Guide to Book Publishing*. New York: Vault, Inc., p. 5.
5. Ibid, p. 13.
6. Ibid.
7. Statistical Abstract of the U.S., 2000, No. 920, Media Usage and Consumer Spending: 1992-2000, www.census.gov prod.99 pubs.99statab/sec18.pdf.

8.  Milliot, J. "Measuring the Salary Divide." *Publishers Weekly*, 7/23/ 2007. www.publishers.weekly.com/article/CA6461981.html?q=salary+survey.

9.  Results of composite AAP Demographics Survey, 6 publishers reporting, October 25, 1999.

10.  Miller, Laura J. (2000). "The Best-Seller list as Marketing Tool and Historical Fiction." *Book History*, Vol. 3; p. 286.

11.  Miller, p.291. [Miller states that because the *Times* won't disclose data, there is no way to check their claim].

12.  Go to http://publishers.org/main/industryStats/indStats_02.htm.

13.  Ibid, p. 81.

14.  Stein, Robert. "Publishing: NameGame." *Newsweek*, MSNBC, January 16, 2006.

15.  Charles, Ron. "Da Vinci Code sets a record, inspires a genre." *The Christian Science Monitor* (www.csmonitor.com) March 19, 2004.

16.  Hackett, A.P., James Henry Burke (1977). *80 Years of Best Sellers, 1895-1975*. New York: R.R. Bowker.

17.  "J.K. Rowling Helps Women Writers Double their Share of #1 Bestsellers, While Male Bestsellers Head for Extinction," (July 20, 2005). www.Lulu.com.

18.  Go to Scholastic.com and "About Scholastic."

19.  Go to www.pearson.com/index.cfm?pageid=16.

20.  "From the typing pool to the boardroom," an interview by Tim Sebastian.

21.  From "Search for Identity, Annenberg Media, American Passages" (1997-2005). Online: Annenberg/CPB.

22.  Interestingly, the BLS refers to African-American women instead of Black.

23.  Workplace Surveys: McGraw-Hill Companies, Inc. Employment Blog: March 23, 2003 (www.vault.com).

24.  www.publishers.org/industry/index.cfm.

25.  The August 27, 2002 report from The Annenberg Public Policy Center of the University of Pennsylvania (Washington).

26.  More information can be found on the Premiere Speakers Bureau's web page: http://premierespeakers.com/joyce_brothers.

27.  "Women in the Labor Force: A Databook." U.S. Dept.of Labor, May 2005, Report 985 (Table 14).

28.  O'Hara, Delia. "Fact: Women know fiction." *Chicago Sun-Times*, November 20, 2005.

# Chapter Four

## The "Muse" in the News: Women and Newspapers

This chapter pertains to newspapers and the industry of the press. We again touch on publishing, but this time it is newspaper publishing that is the focus here.

*FYI—The first time I (Lee) ever saw my name in a byline format of a newspaper was when I was 17 years old. I had written a letter to the editor of The Times Picayune of New Orleans. I don't know why but the editor had called and asked my mother for permission to print it. She got off the phone and said, "Well, Lee, I don't know what you put in the letter to the editor of the Picayune but I do hope the family will not be embarrassed." I waited anxiously the next morning for the paper. I have since then seen my byline on many articles but never again felt that thrill of that morning.*

*FYI—My (Carole's) first experience in the newspaper field was during the New Hampshire primary for the first Bush presidency when he was running against Ronald Reagan. I was working on election coverage for WNEV-TV in Boston and the Middlesex News out of the Framingham suburb asked me to write a human interest article for their Sunday edition about what went on be-hind the scenes at a presidential primary. I had written news for several years by this time and felt pretty confident that the story*

> *would be an easy addition to my work load. I received quite an education when I submitted the article and was called back six different times to add more graphs because I wasn't giving them enough adverbs, adjectives and just plain filler. I realized finally that a print article would have to include everything the viewer in television would see. My AH HA moment.*

What will become of the newspaper is a hot topic today. Many are worried that online news will take over and gone will be the days of the news*paper* with home delivery. Knight-Ridder, an established newspaper publishing company recently sold all of its 32 newspapers; CEO P. Anthony Ridder, claims that profits were just not high enough and stockholders were disenchanted with the newspaper industry. Jon Fine, in his column in *Business Week*, suggests the sale was against Ridder's will.[1] The bottom line is always money.

## Major Newspapers Today

In a report by Journalism.org, the answer to the question, Is the newspaper industry dying? is "Not now." On an average day, they report, roughly 51 million people still buy a newspaper and 124 million in all still read one. The real brunt of bad news comes from the Sunday average reading which has dropped from 73 million in 1990 to 60 million in 2005. Even though circulation is falling, Journalism.org reports that 76 percent of people still read one issue of a newspaper in the course of a week; 50 percent of adults read newspapers daily.[2]

With about 1,450 daily newspapers in the U.S. struggling to stay afloat (and earning 20%-plus profit margin according to Fine), and approximately 7,000 weekly papers still in existence, women continue to find work as reporters and editors. These devotees of the news still believe in objective and fair reporting and themselves as representatives of the public.

## Who Owns the Newspapers?

The top ten US newspapers by circulation include from number one to ten: USA Today (owned by Gannett); Wall Street Journal (owned by News Corp.); New York Times (owned by New York Times Company);

*Los Angeles Times* (owned by The Tribune Co.); *Washington Post* (owned by the Washington Post company); *New York Daily News* and *Chicago Tribune* (both owned by The Tribune company recently taken over by billionaire Samuel Zell); *New York Post* (owned by News Corp.); *Long Island Newsday* (owned by The Tribune company); and *Houston Chronicle* (owned by Hearst Corporation).[3]

The top 22 chains in 2002 (which included Knight-Ridder and the Washington Post Co.), owned 39 percent of all the newspapers in the country (562 newspapers) yet represented 70 percent of daily circulation and 73 percent of Sunday's circulation. In other words, most of the news in daily newspapers came to us from only 22 newspaper company owners in the U.S.[5]

According to the Audit Bureau of Circulations, the top five newspapers with the highest circulations (2004-2005) include *USA Today, The Wall Street Journal, The New York Times, Los Angeles Times* and *The Washington Post*, in that order. Each one of these newspapers is owned by a parent company (often referred to as *media conglomerates* because the parent companies usually own more than newspapers in the mass media category) (See Table 4.1).[6]

# Careers in Newspapers

Newsrooms are shrinking. Between 1999 and 2005, total newsroom work force went from about 58,000 to 57,000, but minority workforce has gone up.[7] Interestingly, medium-sized and small papers are not experiencing severe financial setbacks of the dailies and not cutting staffs. Weekly papers continue to have a bit of edge because they focus strictly on local news and in towns of about 50,000 roughly, local news is very much desired. Career slots then with local newspapers are probably going to stay positive in the next decade. What might eventually impact the weekly is national online news.

National web sites are in for career positions with the big newspapers. *The Wall Street Journal, The New York Times, USA Today* and the *Washington Post* have news staffs of 50 to 100 positions, and smaller city papers are getting very smart. *The Bluffton Today*, which is published out of Bluffton, South Carolina, near Hilton Head, uses reader-contributed material on their participative Web site; *The Dallas Morning News* published both a free youth-targed tabloid and a Spanish-language daily. In the authors' neck of the woods, the Myrtle Beach area of South

Carolina, *The Sun News* (a McClatchy paper) publishes a tabloid geared for the younger crowd called *Surge,* and the younger crowd is talking about it. As innovation becomes greater, so will careers in newspaper venues.

Reporters generally work for newspapers and television or radio and are usually college-trained. Even so, there is a variety of occupations within the industry.

- **Publisher**—This is the person in charge of the entire operation of a newspaper; in daily newspapers owned by major corporations, the publisher is not also the owner; in weekly newspapers, often the owner and publisher is one and the same.
- **Editor**—There is usually one editor in charge, sometimes called the Editor or Executive Editor or Editor-in-Chief. This person is responsible for all the content in a paper. There are also Feature Editors, Senior Editors, Sports Editors and others. All editors work under the main editor (or executive editor) and are usually designed with a subtitle, e.g., features editor, sports editor, entertainment editor, fashion editor, home or living editor, international news editor and more. Editors answer to publishers.
- **Managing Editor**—This person is accountable to the publisher within a newspaper's offices. People in advertising sales, classified sales, special features sales, and news all are accountable to the managing editor. The managing editor reports to the publisher of the paper.
- **Assistant Managing Editor**—This person works directly for the managing editor and sits in on news planning each day as well as budget meetings. This person is in fact involved in every aspect of producing a daily newspaper.
- **Copy Editor**—This person is responsible for clarity and grammatical correctness in a newspaper. Usually a proofreader and a couple of other copy editors work within the supervision of the main copy editor.
- **Columnist**—This person usually has had a long career already as a reporter, editor, or perhaps has held various editorial positions. In other words, one does not apply for a position as columnist, which is an opinion-piece writer, with-

out a vast background in writing for print publications. Often the columnist will be syndicated, which means his or her column is read by other papers on a weekly or daily basis.

- **Reporter**—This person has a degree usually in journalism; sometimes, however, people acquire degrees in other fields then end up pursuing jobs in news-media venues quite by accident. A person with a business degree and a love for writing is an ideal candidate for a reporter assigned to the business beat, for example. It might take that person longer to earn his or her salary simply because there will be so much to learn while on the job. Comparatively speaking, the journalism degreed student will graduate with a portfolio of published pieces, at least from the school paper but additionally from other sources of writing, such as local magazines and newspapers in the vicinity of the college attended.

The above occupations refer to the production of news alone; in addition, there are photographers, layout and graphic designers, production supervisors and press-people who work together to get the paper printed every day. Behind the scenes are all those people who take care of customers, deal with advertisers, and supervise all the clerical staff that any daily newspaper includes.

## Women's Careers in Newspapers

In a column written by Geneva Overholser, for the *Columbia Journalism Review* in 2002, Overholser noted that a study from Northwestern's Media Management Center disclosed that there was an imbalance in top newspaper management jobs with only a handful of women among the 30 or 40 executives who gather for seminars at the school; yet the schoo's journalism classes were more than 70 percent women.[8]

The 2006 "Highlight of Women's Earnings in 2006" report by the Bureau of Labor Statistics discloses that at all levels of education women have fared better than men with respect to earnings growth, and women working full time in management had median weekly earnings of $881 in 2006 which was more than women earned in any other major occupational category.[9] Also, Overholser wrote that the highest positions (president, publisher and CEO), in 137 newspapers with a circulation over 85,000, showed only eight percent were women.[10]

Yet, journalism schools continue to churn out higher percentages of female graduates. The Digest of Education Statistics for 2005 discloses that the graduating class of 2004 included more females than males acquiring bachelor's, master's and doctorates in communications, journalism and related programs. The report by Northwestern mentioned above was published just recently. It discloses that in top level positions at the largest daily newspapers that range from President/Publisher/CEO down to Managing Editors, women numbered 331 versus 908 men in 2003 and 362 women versus 891 men in 2006. Moreover, the number of women at the very top is about one in six. In the top six newspaper groups, The McClatchy company leads with 36% women as publishers (but this means that only 4 of 11 publishers are female). Of the six top newspaper groups, including Lee Enterprises (Pulitzer Inc. is part of this group), there are 272 total publishers of which 72 (or 26%) are female.[11]

Sheila Gibbons (Women's *e*News) reports recently that 37.7 percent of newsroom professionals are women and she reports 29 percent of top managers in newspapers are women.[12] The Bureau of labor Statistics reported for November 2004 that there were a total of 52,730 people employed as reporters and correspondents.[13] This figure does not include all those people who are hired in entry-level positions (e.g., customer service, administrative staff, clerks, etc.). Pam Moreland, assistant managing editor of the *San Jose Mercury News* states that in entry-level jobs, women outnumber men in the newspaper field.[14] Does this mean there is a glass ceiling in place?

In Overholser's column in 2002 (cited above), she reported that when she examined the op-ed pages (Opinion/Editorial pages) of the *Washington Post*, the *New York Times* and the *Los Angeles Times*, she found that there were 88 signed pieces after September 11 tragedy but only five were by women. Yet, women publishers doubled between 2000 and 2003. In a report by Joe Strupp, *Editor & Publisher*, in the 137 daily newspapers with a circulation of more than 85,000, there were 18 percent female publishers. The sad news is that only four of the top 30 circulation papers in 2003 had women publishers.[15]

## Women in Newspapers

Among editors in the top newspapers are Carol Clurman, Senior Editor, *USA Weekend,* Geri Coleman Tucker, Depty Managing Editor, Money Section, *USA Today*, Maralee Schwartz, Deputy Business Editor, *Washington Post*.[16]

Internationally, a foundation called the IWMF (International Women's Media Foundation) presented annual awards in 2007 to three international reporters. Sahar Issa, a reporter in McClatchy's Baghdad bureau received the "Courage Award" in 2007 for her reporting work; Peta Thornycroft who renounced her British citizenship in 2001 and became a Zimbabwean citizen so that she could continue to stay in Zimbabwe as a reporter is a recipient of the 2007 Lifetime Achievement Award; and Lydia Cacho, also a recipient of the "courage" award works out of Mexico for CIMAC news agency who has endured numerous death threats because of her articles about organized crime and pedophilia as another Courage Award winner; and the public will recall hearing about the death of Russian reporter, Anna Politkovskaya who received the Courage in Journalism Award in 2002 and who was killed in 2006 because of her dogged reporting about the Chechnyan war in Moscow.[17]

Janet L. Robinson is president and Chief Executive Officer (CEO) of The New York Times Company. Arthur Sulzberger, Jr., is still the Chairman of the New York Times Company and publisher of *The New York Times* (newspaper). Among the 19 executives, called corporate officers, listed for the Times Company, besides Robinson, are Rhonda L. Bruaer, Corporate Secretary and Senior Counsel; Jennifer C. Dolan, V.P., Forest Products; Ann S. Kraus, V.P., Compensation and Benefits; Catherine J. Mathis,V.P., Corporate Communications; and Laurena L.Emhoff, Assistant Treasurer.[18]

Clearly, Robinson climbed the corporate ladder. She joined the Times Company in 1983, worked her way into management and then held a vice president position in advertising and sales, and later served as senior vice president for operations of The New York Times Company.

In the November 3, 2003 edition of Editor & Publisher, Joe Strupp reported that the number of newspaper publishers had doubled and names some: Denise Palmer, *The Sun* (Baltimore, Md.); Sue Clark-Johnson of the *Arizona Republic* (Phoenix, Az.); Kathy Waltz, *Orlando Sentinel* (Orlando, Fl).; Janice Heaphy, *The Sacramento* (Calif.) *Bee*; Sara Bolton, Hilton Head (S.C.) *The Island Packet*; Jayne Speizer, *The Herald* (Monterey, Calif.); Stephanie Pressley, *Idaho Press-Tribune* (Nampa, Id.); Marcia McQuern, *The Press-Enterprise* (Riverside, Calif.) and Karen Elliott House, *The Wall Street Journal* (New York).

Times are risky for newspapers right now. Sheila Gibbons, Women's eNews writes on July 10, 2006 the following:

At a time when layoffs and buyouts are being implemented at venerable newspapers such as *The New York Times*, *The Washington Post* and *The Wall Street Journal*, even women's small gains in influence are significant.[19]

Pam Moreland, assistant managing editor of the *San Jose Mercury News*, is quoted in the Gibbons piece and has this to say:

> Women outnumber men in entry-level jobs. But when it comes to the prestige beats, the assigning editor ranks, the department heads and upper management, the scales tip back toward the men. . . . The larger the newspaper, the likelihood is that you will find male publishers, male executive editors, possibly a woman managing editor, two or three women in the deputy or assistant managing editor ranks, and two or three women department heads.[20]

Even with the seemingly disparity in positions within newspapers, women can and do succeed in the business.

# How to Get Started in Newspaper Publishing Careers

We're about to sound like an old record stuck in "play" here, but we cannot emphasize enough the value of college. We could name dozens of students who worked at college newspapers and/or took reporting courses that landed them jobs at newspapers. Two English majors acquired jobs while in college as copy editors, a field that is always so needy. As we pointed out above, a copy editor is one who really knows the English language and Associated Press Style of writing and will catch even one space too many in a paragraph. Barring college (and we realize that many cannot afford college), the really hard but possible way to land a job is to hang out at a newspaper office and show the editor good writing skills. A good writer without a college degree is still a good writer. One way to probably get a foot in the door is with a local weekly newspaper; they are always short of money and if a writer will work free to get experience, these papers will give that writer a chance.

# Spotlight

Kathy Ropp is Editor of the Horry Independent, a weekly newspaper owned by Steve Robertson who also published other weeklies in Conway, South Carolina with a combined circulation of more than 20,000. Kathy was born and raised in Conway, S.C., which is located about 10 miles due west of Myrtle Beach. She went to college at the University of South Carolina to study advertising and public relations. Here is how she got started:

*I wanted to be either a copy writer or a media buyer, but I had to take a reporting class for the major. The professor was really tough and I was pretty terrified in his classes. One day he said to me, "Ms. McCaskill (my maiden name then) are you still over in advertising cutting and pasting up ads? I think you should move over here to news." Well, I had no intention of doing that. When my husband, whom I married after college, and I decided to move back to Conway, I worked my way into writing the woman's section of another paper then called the* Field & Herald. *When Steve decided to start* The Independent, *I followed him and within a few years was asked to be editor. So I made it to writing news after all."*

In 1983, Kathy Ropp was the recipient of the South Carolina Newspaper woman of the year.

## Minority Women and Newspaper Careers

While we have been writing about women in this text, we have included all women, which means all minorities as well. Newsrooms, however, at major newspapers (daily circulation of 85,000 or more) are not densely populated with minority women writers.

In the EEOC report filed in 2000, minority women, like white women, at newspapers are more dominant in positions classified as office and clerical workers but fall below in numbers in positions of laborers, technicians and service workers. And in positions classified as officials and managers, minority women number 1,949 (Black women are at 1,098) to white women, 21,785. Men outnumber the women: White men account for 36,994 and minority men account for 3,346 (Black men are at 1,700).

According to the American Society of Newspaper Editors, minority women classified as professionals in newsrooms make up 16.27 percent of the 37 percent of all women professionals in the newsroom. Daily newspaper staffs are still largely male with about ten percent listed as minority men.[21] The EEOC report (with 2004) lumps newspaper, periodical, book and database publishing altogether. The report indicates that there were 518,000 employees, both male and female, with 29,284 classified as Black women; 15,789 as Hispanic women; 8,271 as Asian; and 1,220 as Alaskan native. In an unpublished table of the Bureau of Labor Statistics, for 2005, minority workers in the the entire newspaper industry alone, which means about 1,500 daily papers and 7,000 weekly papers that employed over 500,000, made up only 60,000 (11%). Of the 60,000, Black or African women comprised 19,000 and Asian women comprised 6,000. Still, another survey, this time very recent by ASNE again indicates that minorities account for 11.2 percent of all supervisors in newsrooms; the percentage of minorities (men and women) working at newspapers with more than 500,000 circulations is 16 percent, down slightly from 18.4 percent last year. At newspapers with circulations of 100,000 to 500,000, minorities (men and women) account for 25 percent. Minority women account for 17.55 percent of female newsroom staffers, and 64.5 percent of all supervisors are men.[22]

If all the news we see published is written by mostly white people, with gatekeepers who are white and male, what does this infer in systems theory? It infers, or perhaps precludes, that newspaper publishing as an industry is not quite an open system.

A better question would be what does the glass ceiling look like to minority women who opt for careers in newspapers? The answer may be that not only is the glass ceiling firmly in place, it is opaque in color (i.e., not transparent). In other words, minority women can't even see who's at the top rung of the career ladder.

## Newspapers and the Glass Ceiling

While *USA Today* is under supervisory control by its female president, Sue Clark-Johnson, the *New York Times* (newspaper) is not. Rather the female president and CEO, Janet L. Robinson, is in management for the New York Times Company. The five newspapers shown in Table 4.1 all have men as editors and publishers. The three other women noted are in vice president positions. Interestingly, of the five media corporations mentioned in Table 4.1 only two have female members on the boards: Gannett has 3 women of its 9 directors and Tribune has 2 women of 12 directors.[23] Additionally, the 2004 Census of employed persons discloses that in newspaper publishing, 46 percent employed are women. Can we conclude that if the executives (publishers and editors) at these newspapers are men, then news is going to be centered mostly around men?

A study, published in 2002, of 18 American newspapers that included newspapers from the largest community (New York City) and ranged downward to the smallest community (Fairbanks, Alaska) found that of the 895 stories that were analyzed, the newspaper community, if ethnically diverse, would have more women appearing in the stories. The author concluded that the findings suggest that the more racially diverse the community, the more likely it is to represent women as significant and important newsmakers. Nevertheless, the study also found that males were continually dominant in news coverage overall.[24]

More recently, in another of Sheila Gibbons' columns, Women's eNews, February 22, 2006, she reported that globally, women are the second sex in breaking and making news globally. Here is a quote from her column:

> Monitors for the third Global Media Monitoring Project studied a full day of radio, television and newspaper content in 76 countries on a single day, February 16, 2005. The study found that women continue to be underrepresented, and sometimes outright ignored as subjects of and sources for news, regardless of the medium. There is not a single major news topic in which women outnumber men as newsmakers. "Even in stories that affect women profoundly, such as gender-based violence, it is the male voice (64 percent of news subjects) that prevails," the report released last week in London found.[25]

Not too long ago, newspapers used to include a "Fashion" section that would depict latest fashions and articles about clothing, jewelry, etc. It is probably that ads diminished as more fashion went on air. Still, even if this is the case and fashion just does not have a separate place anymore in newspapers, the fact that studies have found fewer women than men are being used as news quotes and bylines does give us pause for reflection.

In a survey dated September 2002 conducted by the American Press Institute, Pew Center for Civic Journalism, 202 male editors and 72 female editors (at daily newspapers with daily circulations of more than 50,000) responded. Sixty-four (64) percent of the women who saw opportunities limited identified management's preference for the opposite sex as standing in their way. The survey found more job satisfaction from the male respondents than from the females. While both male and female editors responded as being middle-rank managing editors (32 percent), the ratio of those at the bottom (below the managing editor position) to those at the top rank (the position of editor) is greater than 2-to-1 (48 percent). Men are more likely than women to claim knowledge of the business side of newspapers and to motivate others through positive interaction. Women are more likely to have spoken at a national journalism conference and to have served as an officer for a national journalism organization than men. Almost every woman in the survey (90 percent) said she had been asked to handle dirty work for her boss (compared to 79 percent of men).

## Diversified Diva: Erma Bombeck

One of the most interesting diversified divas that began a career in the newspaper business was Erma Bombeck (b.1927) who launched her writing career with the *Dayton Journal-Herald* first as a copygirl and then as a full-time writer. Born into a working class family, saving for college was a must and she began finally three years after high school, in 1947, at Ohio University in Athens, 137 miles away from home. She did not make it on the university's newspaper staff so she left and went back to Dayton enrolling in a four-year Catholic college, the University of Dayton. Her humorous side probably came out while writing for Rike's Department Store's newsletter where she joked about clearance sales, the lunch menu and even shoplifting. Still at the University, a Brother read her articles that she had produced for the school newspaper and asked her to write for the university's magazine. Bombeck graduated from the university in 1949.

Back at the Dayton Journal-Herald she was assigned to the women's section. She started columns in 1952 under the title, "Operation Dustrag" with household hints and product evaluations. She moved forward with an editing job at the Dayton Shopping News and continued with her witty columns. When the family (she was by now married and had two children) moved to Centerville, Ohio, she landed a job as a columnist for $3.00 a week with the Kettering-Oakwood Times, but when the editor of the *Dayton Journal-Herald* saw she was publishing in the Times, he upped her pay to $50.00 per week for two columns; within a short time Newsday Newspaper Syndicate offered to syndicate her columns, which meant that 38 papers were now buying her 400-500 word pieces.

Within five years, her column called "At Wit's End" was syndicated in 500 newspapers; before long she was on a speaker's circuit traveling around and speaking to people who engaged her. She then published a compilation of her columns in a book released in 1967 that she expected would sell big. It did not happen. However, within a short time, she had an agent and published more books. Her book, *The Grass is always Greener Over the Septic Tank*, was a best seller in 1976. She continued to churn out biweekly columns and then started a monthly column in the magazine, *Good Housekeeping*, which continued for six years. She wrote more books that were successful: *Just Wait Til You Have Children of Your Own* (1971) and *I Lost Everything in the Post-Natal Depression* (1974) and her most political one about women and equal rights, *If Life Is A Bowl of Cherries, What Am I Doing in the Pits?* (1978).

Television came calling for Bombeck to be on the *Good Morning America* show where she would talk two or three minutes about life but she later turned into an interviewer with celebrity guests. Her contract last 11 years. Meanwhile, *The Grass Is Always Greener* became a television movie starring Carol Burnett in 1978,but critics hated it. In 1979, ABC asked her to develop a sitcom of her own choosing, which she called Maggie; after 13 episodes, though, the show failed. Before she died in 1996 from a kidney transplant, she wrote, *I Want to Grow Hair, I Want to Grow Up, I Want to Go to Boise*, about children suffering with cancer. The book was about all the funny things that kids with cancer did—the practical jokes and pranks they pulled. The humanitarian Bombeck wanted to let people know that children with cancer are still children. She spent three years among kids and their families at camps developed just for their treatment. She dedicated the American profits from the book to the American Cancer Society and international profits to Eleanor Roosevelt International Cancer Research Fellowships.

Erma Bombeck was 69 years old when she died. [Source: The Erma Bombeck Museum.][26]

# Summary

In a special report published by the EEOC, 2004, about the glass ceiling for women, 60 percent of all workers are women. Yet, women represent only 36 percent of officials/managers but 80 percent of office/clerical workers. Again, newspaper publishers are lumped with book and database publishing in the report and table about managers, which indicates a ratio of 39 percent women.[27]

Still, women college graduates in journalism and related degrees outnumber men graduates. Women can find jobs in newspapers—the position of reporter may be more difficult at larger newspapers for both men and women, but there have been traditionally technical slots predominantly for men and clerical slots predominantly for women. In leadership roles, editor and publisher for example, at the larger newspapers, females are scarce. Even in the parent companies, few women appear in key executive roles (officers and/or members of the boards). While there are close to 1,500 daily newspapers in the country, about 22 corporations own 39 percent of all newspapers in the country (562) as of 2002, but they control 70 percent of daily circulation. And *USA Today* (owned by Gannett) alone has a daily circulation of 2,528,437. Now that Knight-Ridder is no longer part of the top 22 newspaper groups, this means one less conglomerate but a larger slice of dailies for McClatchy.

What is of concern to many people is the fact that news sources (people who are quoted in the news) are mostly male and topics in the news are mostly gendered toward male interests. A review of any Sports section of any daily exemplifies this. Now fashion sections are more or less extinct and women's health issues usually appear in special weekly sections. With regard to minority issues, as one survey indicated, greater volume of news pertaining to diverse groups (minorities) are found in those newspapers within communities that are densely diverse.

Like the world of book publishing, one could offer a charge that because the upper management of the medium of the newspaper is mostly male (and white), content will continue to reflect the taste and culture of the same gender and race. It is a drastic charge and one that is difficult to support without constant data. Too often, as we have noted throughout the text so far, government offices and some private industry organizations lag behind in gathering data or do not always agree. Hence, for example, we are dealing with data about minority employment from a report by the EEOC dated 2002 but Bureau of Labor Statistics data from

2004. What's more is the fact that the EEOC lumps newspaper and book publishing into one category.

While there is fierce competition between broadcast and print news, it appears that like the book in paper form, newspapers somehow continue to survive. We may well see people walking around with the *e*newspaper one day. (Amazon just started marketing Kindle, a handheld electronic book that weighs only 10 ounces). Perhaps they will be paper thin, weigh barely a couple of ounces and wireless and read everywhere. Jon Fine, the media critic quoted earlier in this chapter wrote this opening regarding his attendance at the Newspaper Association of America's annual conference in April 2006:

> [At this year's annual conference, it] looked a lot like America. An America of local monopolists, that is: overwhelmingly white, male, late-middle-aged, and predisposed to wear suits on Sunday, when traveling.

Jon Fine may not have realized how astute his observation is if we relate it to the problem of the glass ceiling for women in newspapers (and all of media). If everyone looks alike and controls the news, it would seem there is indeed a problem.

The very unfortunate news about newspaper is that they are losing money. In the Annual Report on American Journalism published by State of the Media Organization, 2007, between 2005 and 2007, stock decline for the major newspapers was significant: Gannett (-26%), Tribune (-26%), New York Times (-41%), McClatchy Newspapers (-43%); Washington Post (-20%).[28] Glass ceilings or not, newspapers in general are in trouble and digitalized news is just around the corner. If women publishers step in, their task is greater than a male counterpart because they not only have to face any gender bias in the newsroom, they might have to face the facts of an at-risk newspaper.

In the next chapter, we will discuss the world of magazines—careers, occupations, and the glass ceiling.

Table 4.1 Major Dailies

| USA Today | The Wall Street Journal | New York Times | Los Angeles Times | The Washington Post |
|---|---|---|---|---|
| Owned by Gannett Co. Inc. | Owned by News Corp. | Owned by the New York Times Publishing Co. | Owned by the Tribune Publishing Co. | Owned by the Washington Post Co. |
| Gannett's stock price @3/19/08 = $30.24 | News Corp.'s stock price @3/19/08 = $18.84 | New York Times Publishing Co.'s stock price @3/19/08 = $19.08 | Tribune's stock price @3/19/08 = $33.07 | Washington Post Company's stock price @3/19/08 = $654.00 |
| Sept. 15, 1982 | July 8, 1889 | Sept. 18, 1851 | Feb. 1, 1873 | Dec., 1877 |
| Circulation: 2,528,000 | Circulation: 2 million | Circulation: 1,683,800 | Circulation: 1,272,187 | Circulation: 960,600 |
| Publisher: Jeff Webber | Publisher: Robert Thomson | Publisher: Arthur Sulzberger, Jr. | Publisher: Jeffrey Johnson | Publisher: Donald Graham |
| Editor: Ken Paulson | Managing Editor: Marcus Brauchli | Editor: Bill Keller, Exec. Editor | Editor: Dean Baquet | Executive Editor: Leonard Downie |
| Top female position: Sue Clark-Johnson, President, Newspaper Division of Gannett Co., Inc. | Top female position may be: Tina Gaudoin,* named editor of Pursuits, a luxury magazine to start in fall | Top female position: Janet L. Robinson, Pres., and CEO of The New York Times Co. | Top female position: Ruthellyn Musil, Sr. V.P., Corporate Relations, Tribune Co. | Top female position: Diana M. Daniels, V.P., General Counsel and Corporate Secretary |
| Total employed: 52,600 Gannett | Total employed: 7,000 | Total employed: 11,965 NY Times Company | Total employed: 21,000 Tribune | Total employed: 16,400 Washington Post Co. |

Compiled with data from ASNE.org and Morningstar (Yahoo.com). (* There's been a slight shakeup since News Corp. took over the WSJ so this is truly a guess.)

# Notes

1. Fine, Jon. "Life Among the Dinosaurs," *Business Week*, April 17, 2006, p. 24.

2. See www.stateofthemedia.org/2007/.

3. See www.newspapers.com/top10.html.

4. From the Newspaper Association of America (www.naa.org).

5. From "The State of the News Media, 2004" published annually by Journalism.Org. (www.stateofthenewsmedia.org/2007/printable_newspapers_chapter.asp?media=1&cat=1).

6. Ibid. See "Newspaper Company Stock Values, 2004-2005."

7. Ibid, See "Paper Size."

8. See the whole report at www.bls.gov/cps/cpswom2006.pdf.

9. Overholer, Geneva. (2002) "Afer 9/11:Where are the voices of women? CJR.Issue 2:March/April. http://cjrarchives.org/issues/2002/2/girls-over.asp

10. See the whole report at www.bls.gov/cps/cpswom2006.pdf

11. Ibid.

12. Gibbons, Sheila. "Women at Newspaper Helms Face Risky Business," *Women's eNews*, May 11, 2006. (www.womenenews.org).

13. Ibid.

14. Go to www.bls.gov/oes/current/oes273022.htm.

15. Gibbons.

16. Strupp, Joe. "No More Glass Ceiling?" *Editor & Publisher*, Vol. 236, Issue 39, 11/3/2003.

17. These women were named as guests at a Media Relations Summit 2007 in Washington, D.C. by way of Infocomgroup@p.bulldogreporter2.com.

18. Visit the IWMF at www.iwmf.org.

19. www.nytco.com/company-executives.html.

20. Gibbons, S. (2006). "Women at Newspaper Helms Face Risky Business." *Women's eNews*, July 10; published by Maynard Institute, www.maynardije.org/columns/guests/060710_riskybusiness.

21. Ibid.

22. ASNE Survey of April 20, 2004 published online at www.asne.org/index.cfm?id=5145

23. Go to www.asne.og/index.cfm?ID=6264

24. Census of Women Board Directors from April 1, 2004 to March 31, 2005 (www.catalyst.org).

25. Armstrong, Cory. "Papers give women more attention in ethnically diverse communities." *Newspaper Research Journal*, Fall 2002 v.23 i4 p. 81(5).

26. Gibbons, Sheila. "Women's Lowly News Status is a Global Insult." *Women's eNews*, February 22, 2006, (www.womensenews.org).

27. Go to www.ermamuseum.org.

28. This report can be accessed at www.stateofthemedia.org/2007/printable_newspapers_chapter.asp?media=1&cat=1.

# Chapter Five

## That Magazine, There on the Table

> *FYI—I (Lee) sold a magazine article of 150 words to a magazine in the 1970s called Young Athlete. I received a check for $15.00 and framed it. I told my husband then I would become a significant magazine writer. Later, I became editor of a small bimonthly in Augusta, Georgia. The publisher was African-American, a female attorney; I was a part-time instructor at a small university. She and I attempted to include coverage that was equally divided between both races. We worked very hard at it, but the magazine reached its zenith after five years. She tried hard to keep it afloat; I did not take a salary. We both loved the magazine. I like to think I was a significant magazine writer.*

When a magazine reaches its sixth year of publication, the chances are improved that it will have a long life. The word, *magazine*, by the way, comes from the French *magazin*, which really referred to the stockpile of canons at defense forts along coastal areas. The Oxford English Dictionary states this for its definition: A place where goods are kept in store; a storehouse for goods or merchandise; a warehouse or depot.

What is interesting about the word is that people also have a tendency to "stockpile" magazines – you know the ones on the coffee table, or in the bathroom or "over there," stacked on the floor in the corner.

In order to narrow the discussion down a bit, this chapter focuses on the category of *lifestyle*. Women's magazines are included in the category of lifestyle, listed in eighth place among the top 10 types of magazines sold today.

The chapter also focuses on the subject of careers, the number of women employed in the magazine industry and types/content. From this point forward in the chapter, we will refer just to one category of magazines (which will exclude technical, academic and medical journals, and periodicals and include only women's magazines).

The chances are great that most of you reading this text right now subscribe to one or more magazines. Sales (called revenue) are up in subscriptions—$7.2 million in 2004 and $7.4 million in 2005, with total circulation revenue (single copy purchases included) coming in at $10.5 million for year end 2005.[1] Yet, the world of magazines is a crowded one.

## Major Magazines

*Good Housekeeping, Family Circle, Woman's Day, Better Homes and Gardens* and *Ladies' Home Journal* s {labeled lifestyle or women's magazines} are among the top ten magazines in circulation in 2005 according to the MPA (Magazine Publishers of America). (See Table 5.1 appended to this chapter).

Popular magazines for young women include *Cosmopolitan* and for teens, *CosmoGIRL!* and *Seventeen,* which are owned by The Hearst Corporation.

Magazine titles topped 17,000 in 2002; the MPA reports that titles now top 20,000, but the number fluctuates daily as magazines go in and out of business. In an article published on Vault.com's website, Salley Melanie Lourenco writes that "Nowhere is change more a mandate than in the magazine business, especially when it comes to covering the fickle subjects of fashion and celebrity."[2] She claims there are few editors and publishers that can maintain readership through ups and downs of trends in our society. She also claims that women's consumer magazines are the most volatile of a fickle multi-billion dollar industry because so much depends on ad revenue and ads depend on readership and readers want predictions about everything, cosmetics, hair, colors of clothing, shoes, purses and shampoo. Editors have to attempt to figure all of this out. If they can't get hold of the American woman's tempo, they are often ousted. Recently, for example, the former editor in chief of *Harper's Bazaar* was asked to leave on a Thursday and on Friday the former editor of *Marie Claire* took over as editor-in-chief.

One online company, Wooden Horse Publishing,[3] tries to keep up with all press announcements, but recently missed the release about the managing editor of *Ebony* stepping down and being replaced by co-managing editors, Lynn Norment and Walter Leavy. Like Lourenco writes, the magazine world is often chaotic.

The excerpts that follow illustrates the *topsy-turvy* world of magazines. We will review four major magazines: *Redbook, Cosmopolitan, Ms,* and *CosmoGIRL!*. Notice how each one attempts a target audience.

## *Redbook*

*Redbook* was founded in 1929 and owned by McCall Corporation; in 1949 McCall hired a new editor, Wade Nichols Jr. to replace long-time editor, Edwin Balmer. Jump ahead 30 years, 1970 to 1979 when *Redbook,* considered the most intellectual of the Seven Sisters was sold in 1975 to the Charter Co. who turned around and sold it in 1981 to the Hearst Corporation, where it joined *Good Housekeeping* and *Cosmopolitan*. The magazine was always known for its fiction, which comprised 30 percent of each edition and the mature women loved it. When Annette Capone was brought in from *Mademoiselle* as editor, she decided the target should be women in their thirties. She lasted nine years before Ellen Levine, editor of *Woman's Day*, took over *Redbook* in 1991. She tried to restructure it with articles that were not so cozy—"Why I Date Your Husband," "If Sex Hurts. . ."—and stressed beauty and fashion. She was pretty successful and was swooped up in the top editorial spot of *Good Housekeeping* in the fall of 1994; meanwhile, Kate White left *McCall*'s to become *Redbook*'s editor.[4]

Between 1965 and 1975, two almost diametrically opposed women's magazines would take center stage. *Cosmopolitan* began in the early 1900s, did a redesign in 1965, with editor, Helen Gurley Brown (author of the best-selling *Sex and the Single Girl* under her belt) rejuvenating the magazine with self-help and sexuality for the single female, and *Ms Magazine*, a definitively feminist magazine, was launched in 1972 with Gloria Steinem as editor. Clearly, Betty Friedan (author of *The Feminine Mystique*) was not thrilled at the re-shaped Cosmo. Friedan's assessment of the magazine was that of "an immature, teenager-level sexual fantasy based on the ugly and horrible idea that woman is nothing but a sex object."[5] Let's look at these two major magazines: *Cosmopolitan* and *Ms*.

## *Cosmopolitan*

*Cosmopolitan* had actually been around since 1893 and by 1914 it was totally a fictional magazine. Hearst Corporation bought it in 1913 when the company also purchased *Harper's Bazaar*. It somehow managed to stay afloat during three wars and a depression, but just at the dawn of the Vietnam War it began losing circulation and advertising. In stepped Helen Gurley Brown, who had been in advertising and had just authored a best seller titled, *Sex and the Single Girl*. She convinced Hearst to let her transform the magazine. Here is what The National Magazine Company, a United Kingdom online company writes:

> Brown approached Hearst with the idea of creating a new magazine based on the philosophy of her book—advising girls on how to get the best from their lives, jobs and relationships. Hearst shrewdly decided to let Gurley Brown transform the ailing *Cosmopolitan*.[6]

Helen Gurley Brown took the plunge with a first issue under her editorial supervision in 1966 that sold over a million copies. She threw in as much "sexual" content as the times would permit. She created controversy in 1972 when she featured Burt Reynolds as a nude centerfold—but actually his genitalia was covered with a fur coat. The feminists were in an uproar.

By 1990, *Cosmopolitan* had grown from sales of 800,000 to 2.5 million and became the sixth best-selling newsstand magazine in any category. In January 1996, after 32 years as editor-in-chief, Helen Gurley Brown stepped down and was replaced by Bonnie Fuller, founding editor of *Marie Claire*. Brown's eighth book, *I'm Wild Again: Snippets from My Life and a Few Brazen Thoughts* was published; it is filled with information on her face lifts, staying thin, and how to keep a man and succeed in a career. Her key to success: work harder than anyone else.

## *Ms.*

The first issue was launched in January, 1972 and was published as a monthly until 1987. It was then bought by an Australian media company in 1989 and began publishing without any ads. In 1998 it was published by Liberty Media which was operated by the magazine's first editor, Glorida Steinem. Since 2001 it has been owned by the Feminist Majority Foundation headed by Eleanor Smeal.

*Ms.* took issue with inequality for women. The magazine was called "a feminist magazine" by critics, as if the word, feminist, were something like a disease. If feminist meant rebellion, then women were indeed feminists. They were burning their bras while young men were defecting to Canada. It was the time of the flower-child and hippies who thought life was a "trip." It was the beginning of the quest for an equal rights amendment and *Ms.* helped a lot with balanced reporting and well-known writers. Gloria Steinem, who looked anything but militant, became very popular by women who sought liberation but not by women who applauded the homemaker and the fact that business was a man's world. The fact is that the world was a man's world, and many would argue still is.

The title of *Ms.* magazine came from the then-current controversy over the "correct" title for women. Men had "Mr." which gave no indication of their marital status; etiquette and business practices demanded that women use either "Miss" or "Mrs." Many women did not want to be defined by their marital status, and for a growing number of women who kept their last name after marriage, neither "Miss" nor "Mrs." was technically a correct title in front of that last name.

*Ms. Magazine*, which advocated women with brains, and *Cosmopolitan*, which advocated women as sex objects, could not have been more diametrically opposite. Clearly there was no love lost between Gloria Steinem and Helen Gurley Brown, whether or not they would admit it.

Today, *Ms.* remains in publication, Ms.com, but it is not in the top 100 in circulation sales.

## Seventeen

The title is taken from a novel by Booth Tarkington (1869-1946) and began publishing in 1944. BookRags.com states that the Tarkington novel, *Seventeen:A Tale of Youth and the Baxter family, Especially William*,was required reading for generations of high school students. The target, however, from the beginning was teenage girls and was the first devoted to the needs and likes of adolescents, more specifically to young people and fashions, beauty, movies and music. The founding editor was Helen Valentine. Circulation jumped from one million in 1947 to 2.5 million by 1949; at the turn of the 21st Century,it remained the most widely read magazine among teen girls. Magazine Publishers Association (MPA) reports it as number 31 for 2005 in the top 100 circulated magazines.[7]

According to Nancy Walker, *Seventeen* prepared younger women for young adulthood; one article published in 1944 titled,"What Are You Doing about the War?" applauded young teens for volunteer work and some type of training, in nursing or flight attendants in aviation and in child care work after the war.[8] It was not unusual to find cake baking ideas in these early editions for teen girls were expected to inherently want to be experts in the kitchen. In the January,1948 issue, under "Cutting a Cook's Corner," the author recommended a pantry stocked with canned paté, dehydrated soups, biscuit mix, and canned roast chicken.[9] This of course is a far cry from today's cover stories such as "Hair Bliltz: The best bangs for your face!", "Best Friends for Never?", "How to deal when you grow apart!", "I'm 13 and my boyfriend is hinting about sex", or "Sex Smarts: Think you're ready to have sex?" No recipes show up on this online *Seventeen* cover dated 6/23/06.[10]

## CosmoGIRL!

As incredible as it sounds, Hearst Corporation, already publishing *Seventeen* Magazine launched *CosmoGIRL!* in 1999, becoming the first teen magazine to include a financial section and praising young female entrepreneurs each month. It began with a "virginal" tone to it but one reviewer states that the magazine does everything but market sex to its audience of 12- to 17-year-olds. One cover in 2005 had a sexy, bosomy Lindsay Lohan featured and a tell-all in the contents, plus the issue offered "5 Flirting Secrets That'll Make Him Want You Bad." The magazine today is not at all what Altoosa Rubenstein, its founding editor, said when interviewed in 1999, she said, "We don't use sexy images, and we don't have stick-skinny models. . . . We are about empowering girls." In 2005 the magazine reached a circulation of 1.4 million, and it was launched when there were supposedly 17 teen magazines already on the market.[11]

These magazines, except *Ms*, illustrate the glitz and glamour that women, of all ages, look for in their subscriptions to lifestyle magazines. This does not mean other magazines do not do well.

# Who Owns the Top Magazines?

The top magazines in terms of circulation revenue are: AARP, The Magazine; AARP Bulletin; Reader's Digest; TV Guide; Better Homes and Gardens; National Geographic; Good Housekeeping; Family Circle; Ladies' Home Journal; and Woman's Day.[12] We'll take a close look at the owners of these magazines first. These magazines are all in the hands of CEO/corporate level males according to the parent corporation for each magazine. The major corporations with magazines that target women consumers in their lifestyle category are as follows:

## Meredith Corporation

Meredith Corporation publishes 26 subscription magazines that include in the lifestyle group:

- *Better Homes and Gardens*
- *Ladies' Home Journal*
- *Family Circle*
- *Parents*
- *More*
- *Fitness*
- *American Baby*

According to their corporate web page, there are six corporate (CEO, presidents, CFO, General Counsel and Corporate Controller) officers; none is a woman. However, in its Women's Lifestyle Group according to the 2005 Annual Report, pictured are four females in top positions (Editor-in-Chief of *Ladies' Home Journal*; Publisher of *More*; Senior Vice President and Editor-n-Chief of *More*). In its Parenthood Group are pictures of three women and one man (the male is listed as an executive Vice President and the women as editors). We see almost an even amount of women and men in its Home and Family Creative Group; in the Special Interest Publications (Family and Food Collection, Decoration and Design, Garden), there are three women and one man pictured in editorial roles. Altogether listed for the groups in editorial control of magazines for Meredith are 14 females and 7 males. (We will discuss this further later on).

## Hearst Corporation

Hearst Corporation publishes 17 magazines, many newspapers, owns many television, cable and radio stations, and more. Among the magazines are these lifestyle magazines:

- *Harper's Bazaar*
- *House Beautiful*

- *Good Housekeeping*
- *Redbook*
- *Cosmopolitan*
- *CosmoGIRL!*
- *O, The Oprah Magazine*
- *Marie Claire*
- *Seventeen*

According to the Hearst Corporation's web page (February, 2008) the lineup in the corporate division is 11 men and one woman, the president of the magazine division is Cathleen Black, a female, and Ellen Levine is listed as the Editorial Director, Hearst Magazines; magazine management also includes one other woman, Scherri Roberts, Vice President, Human Resources. So in magazine management there are six men and two women. The magazine editors division is overwhelmingly female: 14 females and four males; the magazine publishers division is overwhelmingly female as well: 10 females and six males. Again, though, we are interested in the clout positions. At Hearst, in clout (corporate and magazine management divisions) there are 17 managers, three are female. Counting these positions and all other divisions with magazine management power there a total of 24 men and 27 women. It is far different in the newspaper divisions.

## Hachette Filipacchi Medias

Hachette Filipacchi Medias (based in France) publishes 18 magazines in North America, more than 45 in France and a few internationally. Among their U.S. magazines in the lifestyle group are:

- *Elle*
- *Elle Décor*
- *Metropolitan Home*
- *Home*
- *Woman's Day*

In its U.S. branch, it has two female executives listed among 14 vice-presidents, one chairman and one president.

# Careers in Magazines

Top heavy with men in clout positions or not, women seek jobs if not as writers/editors than as fashion magazine models. Criticism of content is vast with respect to models and the medium of the magazine is hit the hardest with promotion of a surreal fantasy woman. Scholars have done research about self-perception on the part of female (and male) magazine readers and have found correlation between what women read and the desire to be thin[13] or the belief that a beautiful body means wealth, power and confidence[14] Criticism of magazines like *Good Housekeeping, Family Circle, Parent's* is about the maternal contradictions, e.g., articles that contain messages that promote motherhood and also fault the mother who stays at home.[15] The same types of criticism have been offered with regard to television and the surreal or fantasy people and places presented.

Still, people opt for a career in magazines. Imagine a chance to be part of the team that puts together your favorite magazine—*Elle, Cosmopolitan, O, House Beautiful*, etc., or that puts your face on the cover.

According to the Bureau of Labor Statistics, which track occupations, growth is going to be steady but slow in periodicals (magazines and journals) to the year 2014. We'll take a look now at what they write about employment in periodicals as of 2004.

# Women's Careers in Magazines

Fashion is a major component of most women's magazines. Whether white or any minority, if you have the right look and are, for the most part, pencil-stick thin, you can try for a modeling career. In the fashion industry's career as a model, the 2004 Census report discloses that there were 68,000 people employed as models, demonstrators and product promoters. Of that number, 86.4 percent were women, 8.5 percent of whom were Black or African American, 2.9 percent were Asian and 7.2 percent were reported as Hispanic or Latino.

As we indicated earlier, of all mass media careers, it is the medium of magazine publishing that employs more women than men. In an unpublished report by the Bureau of Labor Statistics for 2005, total employee count was at 302,000 with 156,000 women and 146,000 men. Most of the industry employees are White women (136,000) and likewise White men (124,000).[16]

The BLS list of occupations in magazine publishing include:

- **Writing and Editing**—Correspondents, editors, copywriters.
- **Production occupations**—Production and planning clerks, prepress technicians, printing machine operators (still needed because everything sent to press room digitally but the press is still very much a part of the operations).
- **Sales, promotion and marketing**—Advertising sales agents generate most of the revenue for newspapers and magazines and even broadcast, although broadcast stations if they are affiliates do get revenue from the networks.
- **General administration occupations**—General managers, accountants, computer specialists and business operations specialists, stock clerks, order fillers, customer service representatives.

# Spotlight

Olessa Pinkak is the beauty editor for *Natural Health* in New York City. She says that one can make it in the magazine business with determination.

*I started out in magazine journalism in 2001. I had graduated from college in May and after a 6-week stint waitressing and living in a share house in Newport, RI, I went to New York City to attend the Columbia Publishing Course. At that time, I thought that I would go into political journalism. I had interned at the Hartford Courant in college, studied abroad in London and interned at a small publication for MP's there, and also interned for various lobbying groups at the capitol in Hartford. After the intensive 8-week course at Columbia, I was interviewing like crazy, taking a broad look at all different types of jobs in the industry. At the end of the job search, my decision had boiled down to two options—work for a political magazine in D.C. or work in New York City for Allure Magazine. It was probably a crossroads in my career, but ultimately, the glamour and intrigue of working for such an esteemed company as Conde Nast beat out the smaller political magazine, no matter how interested I was in the topic. My experience at Allure laid a very solid groundwork for my career in magazines.*

# How to Get Started in
# Magazine Publishing Careers

The chances for jobs are greater if you move to New York City or Boston, where so much of the editorial positions are located, but competition in landing a job is immense. Like so many college students in the area of New York, you would have to try for an internship first to even get on the potential employee list. If it is as a writer you would wish for a job, too, you would have to have a sizeable portfolio of published work already lined up. In other words, getting hired in a major magazine is not impossible but the road is tough. How do you begin a portfolio? Start writing for a local magazine, any magazine, and build a portfolio of articles. Then branch out and send queries to major magazines that accept queries (so many of them state, "No unsolicited articles accepted" which means, don't send us something we don't ask for). Buy a copy of *The Writer's Market* (published annually and always for sale at the big book stores).

However, the glossy magazine world is a crowded one, and it may seem unimaginable for anyone to attempt to create a new one. Yet, people try it all the time even though the life span of a magazine is less than five years. This seems to be the pivoting year for publishing a magazine without profit. If the magazine is not in the black, profit, by the fifth year, it usually folds. Years ago, there used to be movie magazines featuring large head shots of stars; kids would buy them and cut out the pictures and trade them. We still have the celebrity craze today in magazines about music, film and television industries. Yet, what is surprising to find is that the major women's magazines feature so many celebrity interviews.

Mary Ellen Zuckerman points out that it surprises her too considering the amount of celebrity interviews we find available[17] (*People* and *TV Guide* for example). The other problem is that serious subjects, e.g., women continue to earn less per dollar than men or women in higher education may call the shots at a dean's level but rarely at a president's level, are more or less over-shadowed by topics about sexuality, sex, beauty and allure.[18] Who is to blame? Are editors at these women's magazines who are mostly women so caught up in the profit margin that they spend no time in reflection or is it that if serious subjects were inserted into the lifestyle genre, women would stop reading them? It is too easy to blame men at the top of the corporate ladder for women's tastes, and we want to make it clear in this text that this is not what we do. It is a concern that men control the purse strings in mass media, and it is a concern that more women are not on the boards of the big conglomerates, and it is obvious that there is a glass ceiling in place for all women, especially for minority women. That is the point of our text.

# Minority Publishing: African Americans

There are quite a few minority magazines being published today. Target Market News, the Black Consumer Market Authority has articles on its web page dated June 21,2006 about *ONYXStyle* magazine, *Jones*, a new magazine for African-American women, also about *Black Enterprise, JET, Vibe, Essence, Ebony,* and a new one called *VibeVixen*, a beauty and fashion title for women from the publishers of *Vibe*. Together, *Ebony* and *JET* pulled in almost $50 million in ad revenue for 2005.[19]

Johnson Publishing, worth $350 million with 2,000 employees, is the largest black-owned publishing firm in the world. Its holdings include *Ebony* (a monthly) and *JET* (a newsweekly), which together are read in half the black households of America. Linda Johnson is the CEO of both Johnson Publishing and Fashion Fair Cosmetics, the largest black-owned cosmetics firm in the world, with 2,500 stores on three continents.[20]

John H. Johnson, the founder, launched *Ebony* in 1945 and *JET* in 1951. Both have had 50-year runs. Just as we have seen an under-representation of minority women in careers within media, so too has there been an under-representation of minority women in popular press, magazines and newspapers. Minority magazines, like minority newspapers spring from this void. *Ebony* especially has had tremendous success and the Johnson Company diversified into Fashion Fair Cosmetics, the world's number one line of makeup and skin care for women of color sold in over 2500 stores across the U.S. and several countries. *Ebony* (ranked 55 in top100 magazines) is a general black-oriented picture magazine that deals primarily with contemporary topics—about education, history politics, literature, art, business, personalities, civil rights, sports, entertainment, etc. *JET* (ranked 97 in the top 100 magazines) is a weekly that covers mostly general news topics, and Senior Editor, Sylvia Flannigan and Managing Editor, Malcom West, say that the purpose is to inform, educate and entertain Black Americans.

Linda Johnson Rice was appointed president and CEO of Johnson Publishing Company in 2002. Rice is sought after as a speaker by many and has received several awards including the Women of Power Award from the National Urban League, the Trumpet Award from Turner Broadcasting, the Alumni Merit Award from the University of Southern California and others. The company's headquarters is in Chicago with additional offices in New York, Washington, DC, Los Angeles, Detroit and London.

Another successful African American woman is Oprah Winfrey (a *diversified diva*), CEO of Harpo Productions. The company owns all of the Oprah Winfrey shows, and is purported to have annual revenues of about $150 million with about 200 Chicago employees.[21] In an interview with *Fortune* magazine in 2005, the interviewer, Patricia Sellers, states that Oprah likes to think of herself not as a businesswoman; yet, she is credited with the success of her company. While Hearst Corporation owns *O, The Oprah Magazine,* Oprah Winfrey calls the shots. (We talk more about Oprah in the television chapter).

## Latino/Latina Magazines

President Bush may be still trying to get Congress to pass the guest worker visa program for Latinos to work in this country, but the magazine industry is taking full advantage of the fact that they are already here.

According to an article about a study of Latina magazines, which means the researcher studied magazines that targeted Latina women, the world's largest publisher of Spanish-language magazines is Editorial Televisa, in Mexico City with U.S. operations in Miami. Newstands regularly sell these magazines, some of which are U.S. majors like *Cosmopolitan*, *Glamour*, *Marie Claire*, *Good Housekeeping* and *Harper's Bazaar*, in Spanish. One Spanish-language produced magazine is *Vanidades* (a 37 year old upscale women's magazine); *Latina Style*, *Moderna* and *Latina Bride* are recent publications. Their study looked at 601 items/articles in the content of the last four mentioned above; 20% were personality features, 20% devoted to beauty and fashion and five percent (5%) was each devoted to romance and sex, careers and education and health. More serious issues, such as diversity issues in education, government, the workplace or society totaled just 3% of the coverage. *Latina Bride* was devoted to *quinceañeras*, the 15th-birthday celebration for young women. In short, these researchers conclude that the content was fairly vapid and void of any cultural content.[22]

Coincidentally, in a short *Newsweek* piece, March 27, 2006, the announcement of a new magazine was made that targeted the young teenage 15 year old girls, who will be getting ready to celebrate their quinceañeras. The magazine will be called *Quince Girl*, pronounced "keensay" like the number 15 is pronounced in Spanish. Features will include lots of fashion including gowns, photographers, cakes, and limos, all part of the 15th birthday celebration, which in some cases is more celebrated in the Latina community than their wedding with regard to costs.

Fashion is always center stage in young women's magazines especially, and many young women find themselves drooling over the glamorous and very slim fashion models in magazines. It is as difficult to climb the fashion modeling ladder as it is the corporate ladder, however.

## Magazines and the Glass Ceiling

The 2002 Equal Employment Opportunity Commission's report for periodicals (aka magazines and journals) does not depict a disparity for women but rather for men in the numbers who are (1) officials and managers and (2) professionals.

With a ratio of 26% women and 22% men, women can hardly claim the existence of a glass ceiling, or can they? Remember, a glass ceiling depends on clout positions—people in power positions. As we have seen in most of media, there are few women as corporate executives, CEOs, presidents and few on the boards of these media conglomerates.

Our goal here is to look at corporations that publish women's magazines in order to fully make a determination about the glass ceiling.

It becomes apparent as we go through these chapters that the few women who are named "President" or "Senior Vice President" are women who somehow broke through the glass ceiling. Certainly, magazines is the first medium that we see that is heavily populated with female employees (55%), but as editors and officials and managers and professionals (26%), they are all still reporting to men, mostly white men, firmly at the top. Another look at the EEOC report indicates that 19% of women work in the office. This leaves 10% of women working in fields as technicians (2%), sales (only 7%), craftworkers (.06%), operatives (.01%), laborers (.02%) and service workers (.02%) for a total of 55%. Men, comprising 45% of the employees in magazines and journals, also work mostly as professionals and officials and managers (22%), with the rest, (23%), spread out among the remaining seven categories just mentioned.

Remember, in deciding whether there is a glass ceiling in place, think about the fact that there is only one female president (Cathleen Black at Hearst Corporation) of magazines among the three above.

Editors report to publishers, and publishers report to Corporate Vice Presidents or Presidents. We found the editors' names easily, but it was difficult to determine the publishers of the various women's magazines. Every magazine like newspapers has a publisher who oversees the entire operation. While editors-in-chief are mentioned and shown in groups, both men and women, finding out the names of the publishers and/or associate publishers was almost impossible. For example, in a press release in the *New York Times*, it indicated that Winthrop Stevens, a male, was named as publisher of *Family Circle*. The piece is dated December 7,1989. It is hard to imagine that with the changeable magazine world, Stevens is still publisher. A further search of the Hearst Corporation and the *Family Circle* web pages could still not reveal the publisher's name. In fact, it is quite useless to go to any of the magazines online because they are tabloids not corporate-based informative sites. Meanwhile, at *Better Homes & Gardens,* a copy of the magazine itself lists Carol DeWulf Nickell, Vice President and Editor-in-Chief and Daniel M. Lagani, Vice President and Publisher.

So while Meredith now owns three of the largest of the lifestyle magazines, and while they seem to have many women listed in their corporate web pages, not all information is disclosed—publisher names for example. Is there a glass ceiling at Meredith? Remember systems theory calls for open doors. Someone knows, but not us.

# Diversifed Diva: Martha Stewart

*We repeat, glass ceilings do not exist for divas.*

While Martha Stewart may not be a favorite to all people, clearly she is a favorite to many; otherwise, her success as a diva in magazine and book publishing, television, dinner-music CDs, and her countless other enterprises would not be successful. The public, her public, sees in Martha Stewart a smart entrepreneur who literally carved her way into a fortune.

In 1995, Stewart was inducted into the Academy of Achievement, a museum of living history established in 1961 that honors people who succeed in making a difference in society. Her biography is published on their website[23] and portrays an amazing and active woman—taught to garden by her father, Edward Kostyra, and taught to cook, bake and sew by her mother, Martha Kostyra; she attended Barnard College, worked as a model, married Andrew Stewart a law student, continued to model even doing TV commercials and then became a stockbroker in 1967. She restored an 1805 farmhouse that she and her husband bought in Westport, CT in 1973 where she still lives and in 1976 started a catering business which she ran out of the farmhouse; within 10 years it became a $1 million company. While she first wrote articles for the New York Times, her experience as an editor for *House Beautiful*, we are sure, gave her much of the experience she would later use when launching her own magazine, *Martha Stewart Living*. We decided to spotlight her in the magazine chapter because of the tremendous success of the magazine and at the same time spotlight the entrepreneurial skills of Stewart. Her company, Martha Stewart Omnimedia, Inc. (MSO), has branches in publishing, television, merchandising and internet/direct commerce and provides products in eight areas that range from the home to child care, and what better place to advertise the MSO products than in her own magazine. Circulation was ranked at number 27 with a 2.4 million circulation base in the top 100 magazines when it dramatically dropped in 2001 because of the scandal; today it is ranked number 35 and has a 1.95 million circulation.

Nevertheless, this diva made it through a very tough period in her life in 2003-2005 when she was tried and found guilty of misleading federal investigators and obstructing an investigation; the charges of insider trading were dropped. She spent five months in a minimum security prison and was released on March 3 (a 45-minute ride to her home). On her web page, www.marthastewart.com, she states that the incarceration was "life altering" and she was "thrilled to be returning to my more familiar life." We can only imagine how much of a jolt it was in her life. In any case, she is back. Since her release in March 2005, she has published two more books and her stock has risen (although slightly) from its weakest of $5.00 a share when the scandal broke in 2003 to today's $6.83 per share on the New York Stock Exchange.[24]

We'll probably see lots more of the Martha Stewart brand in the future.

# Summary

Women's magazines, known as lifestyle magazines, are still among the top 10 in circulation with five of them now in circulation for 100 years or more. In magazines, like newspaper and book publishing, a few media conglomerates own the major (top selling) magazines. The magazine or periodical business is slightly chaotic with editorial changes taking place almost daily and new magazines coming out, while old magazines die off. It is difficult then to count the number of magazines in existence at any one time. It could be 17,000 or 20,000.

In the magazine, lifestyle, industry, we find more female employees than men, even more vice presidents in the corporate levels but still there are no CEOs in the top ten. Minority women in the magazine industry are again really a minority with perhaps two glass ceilings.

For some unexplained reason, even though we live in a highly technological and dynamic society, people still want the glossy magazine lying around the house. Even magazines published for minorities continue to do well and now more Latino/a-targeted magazines are surfacing.

There continues, however, to be criticism of magazine content with idealistic glamorous depictions of celebrities or pencil stick-thin models, all of whom create for the reader, especially the young and impressionable, fantasies of a surreal world.

Regardless of the employee count with respect to top level positions for women, another concern that could be more serious is the lack of females on the boards of these conglomerates. For the three mentioned in this chapter, Meredith, Hearst and Hachette Filipacchi, while board members combined totaled 41, only seven were women. Is that why we don't see enough stories about serious female issues in these lifestyle magazines?

### Table 5.1 Top 10 Magazines in Circulation Numbers

| Rank | Publication | 2006 Paid Circulation in Millions | Owner/s |
|---|---|---|---|
| 1 | AARP The Magazine | 23,250,882 | AARP Organization |
| 2 | AARP Bulletin | 22,621,079 | AARP Organization |
| 3 | Reader's Digest | 10,094,284 | Reader's Digest Assn., Inc. |
| 4 | Better Homes & Gardens | 7,627,046 | Meredith Corporation |
| 5 | National Geographic | 5,072,478 | News Corporation |
| 6 | Good Housekeeping | 4,675,281 | The Hearst Corporation |
| 7 | Ladies Home Journal | 4,136,462 | Meredith Corporation |
| 8 | Time—The Weekly News Magazine | 4,082,740 | Time Warner |
| 9 | Woman's Day | 4,014,278 | Hachette Filipacchi Medias (France) |
| 10 | Family Circle | 4,000,887 | Meredith Corporation |

From Circulation Trends and Magazine Handbook, Average Circulation for Top 100
ABC Magazines 2006; www.magazine.org/circulation/circulation_trends_and_
magazine+handbook/22175.cfm

# Notes

1. Data from Magazine Publishers of America (MPA),Combined Circulation Revenue for magazines tracked by the Audit Bureau of Circulations (ABC)
1988-2005 (www.magazine.org).

2. Lourenco, Sally Melanie (2005). Musical Chairs: Movement in the World
of Magazines. Go to: www.vault.com/nr/main_article_detail.jsp?article_
id=10359422&ht_type=5.

3. Go to: www.woodenhorsepub.com.

4. Zuckerman, Mary Ellen (1998). *A History of Popular Women's Magazines in the United States, 1792-1995*, p. 220.

5. Zuckerman, p. 226.

6. Go to www.natmags.co.uk. The website belongs to the National Magazine Ccmpany and offers national magazines timelines and lots of useful in-

formation. The piece about Cosmopolitan focuses mostly on the launch of the UK edition in 1972.

7. Moran, Edwards. "Seventeen." *BookRags*. Retrieved 23 June 1006, from the World Wide Web. www.bookrags.com/history/popculture/seventeen-bbbb-03.html.

8. Walker, Nancy A. (2000). *Shaping Our Mother's World (American Women's Magazines)*. Jackson, MS: University of Mississippi Press; p. 89.

9. Ibid, p. 131.

10. Go to www.seventeen.com.

11. This information comes from a company called BPA worlwide, a company owned by Access Intelligence. Read about all of this on www.minonline.com.

12. Magazine Publishers Association; Average circulation for Top 100 ABC Magazines, 2005 ranked in paid circulation (www.magazines.org/circulation/circulation_trends_and_magazines_handbook/16117.cfm).

13. Park, Sung-Yeon (2005). "The Influence of Presumed Media Influence on Women's Desire to be Thin." *Communication Research*, Vol 32, No. 5, October, p. 609.

14. Woodstock, Louise (2001). "Skin Deep, Soul Deep: Mass Mediating Cosmetic Surgery in Popular Magazines,1968-1998." *Communication Review*, 4:422.

15. Johnston, Deirdre D. and Debra H. Swanson (2003). "Undermining Mothers: A Content Analysis of the Representation of Mothers in Magazines." *Mass Communication & Society*, 6 (3), 246.

16. Unpublished data obtained from the Bureau of Labor Statistics, Employed and Experienced Unemployed Persons by detailed industry, sex, race and Hispanic or Latino ethnicity, annual Average 2005 (Source: Current Population Survey).

17. Zuckerman, p. 235.

18. Ibid, p. 181.

19. According to Publishers Information Bureau of MPA, quoted in TargetMarket News (targetmarketnews.com/magazines.htm).

20. John H. Johnson founded the company in 1942 with his magazine, *Negro Digest*. (www.johnsonpublishing.com).

21. www.encyclopedia.chicagohistory.org.

22. Johnson, Melissa A. (2000). "How Ethnic Are U.S. Ethnic Media: The Case of Latina Magazines." *Mass Communication & Society*, 3 (2&3), p. 235.

23. Click onto Select Achiever then scroll down to Martha Stewart. www.achievement.org/autodoc/page/ste0int-1 < http://www.achievement.org/autodoc/page/ste0int-1 > .

24. See Morningstar quote for Martha Stewart Living Omnimedia, Inc. March 5, 2008: http://quote.morningstar.com/Quote/Quote.aspx?pgid=hetopquote&ticker=MSO&referid=SP018&ss=bc&kw=MSO.

# Chapter Six

# The Back Lot of Movies

*FYI—I (Carole) first worked as line producer, production manager and assistant director on an independent movie called Fried Clams. It was shot on Nantucket Island during the tourist season. We had to shoot overnight in the restaurant owned by the director after it closed for business. After the first week of shooting, when the lighting crew had just unloaded their equipment from the ferry, the financier ran out of money and filming was shut down. The yellow t-shirt "I survived Fried Clams" is all I have left from the experience.*

In this chapter we examine the women who choose to work in the film industry—those who find great stories and adapt them for the big screen, those who develop those stories into *greenlights*, executing the stories from paper into pictures on film, and those who take direction in how to carry-out the storyline into magnificent performances.

## Major Movie Studios

Universal Studios, the oldest studio in Hollywood, was started by Carl Laemmle in 1915. The following year Adolph Zukor, founder of the Famous Players Film Company merged with Jesse Lasky and formed Paramount Pictures. A few years later Harry and Jack Cohn changed their film company's name to Columbia Pictures. Samuel Goldwyn wanted to join these thriving entities and joined with Marcus Loew's Metro Film Company and producer Louis B. Mayer to form MGM Studios which became the most powerful studio in Hollywood. Around the same time Sam Warner and his brothers Harry, Jack and Albert opened Warner Brothers Studio. Harry and Albert remained in New York to deal with financiers and distributors, while Sam and Jack headed to Hollywood to produce pictures. Walt Disney was just a young man when he convinced his brother Ray to join him in their uncle's garage to begin their movie careers at Disney Studios. And in 1935, Daryl Zanuck launched 20th Century Fox at the age of 33.[1]

It was nearly sixty years later (1994) before anyone tried to repeat such a feat. Steven Spielberg, Jeffrey Katzenberg and David Geffen formed Dreamworks, SKG. They were referred to as the dream team. Today their dreams have become great memories.

## Who Owns the Studios?

Over the last forty years the studios have gone through many owners. Electronics companies and liquor companies decided there was money to be made in the movie business and they wanted a stake in that fortune. They discovered that movies alone would not bring in those fortunes, but synergy could make it happen. So they not only own the movie studios, but television stations and magazines, as well as internet sites. This allows them to promote one another through their different vehicles and buffer any shortfalls the same way.

Today Columbia Pictures and MGM are now owned by Sony, Warner Brothers Pictures is owned by Time Warner, Universal Studios is now owned by NBC-Universal (after the liquor company bought and sold), Paramount Pictures and Dreamworks are owned by Viacom and Fox is owned by News Corp.

## Careers in Movies

In the history of movie careers, getting to the "back lot," was the pinnacle of success. It meant that an actor was going to be involved in a major film production, for it was in the back lot where so many films were made and sets transformed into the wild west, or an old New England street or a Renaissance courtyard. If we use the term, back lot, instead, as a metaphor for behind-the-scenes, women would account for only 16 percent of all executive producers, producers, directors, writers, cinematographers, and editors on the top 250 grossing films of 2004.

This means that behind-the-scenes, being on the back lot, is not very much of a pinnacle for women who are not actors.[2]

The Bureau of Labor Statistics reports that in 2004, there were about 368,000 wage and salary jobs in the motion picture and video industries. Occupations include employment in:

- **Producing**—Producers are the first line of defense. They represent the studios and try to make sure the writer's interests are preserved. They hire the director and are responsible for the overall production.
- **Directing**—Directors work for the producer of the film, but are responsible for the creativity and execution (how it looks on screen) of the story. They are intimately involved with casting and working with the actors on set. An accomplished director will be allowed "final cut" of the movie.
- **Casting**—Casting directors and agents are sent call sheets and scripts by the producers in order to find the right person for each role. Some casting directors breakdown these sheets and develop production books for each movie in order to accomplish their goal. Auditioning the right actors or undiscovered talent can sometimes require travel around the country.
- **Acting**—Male and female hopefuls from Broadway and theatrically trained students from around the country flock to New York and Los Angeles to pursue careers on the large and small screens. Actors can experience profit one year and pursuit the next. It is one of the most volatile careers in the industry.
- **Editing**—A crucial behind-the-scenes person is the editor. He or she will spend months editing the film, ordering retakes, mixing sounds via sound studios, calling in the actors on the film to redo their own voices (this is called looping). This person works very closely with the director so as not to change the essence of the film.
- **Screenwriting**—This occupation involves preparing treatments, outlines, drafts, writes and rewrites of the movie script. Many writers spend their early careers as "readers" for studios or production companies. This allows them to see what studios are buying and also shows them how many hundreds

of scripts are received each week and how many never make it beyond the coverage stage. (That's when a reader will prepare a synopsis of the script for the studio executive)

- **Cinematographers**—These craft people compose film shots according to the mood of the director. They are sometimes referred to as the DP (Director of Photography). Most who are worth their weight are considered real artists.
- **Gaffers**—The gaffers are lighting technicians and they work for the person directing all the photography for the film.

# Women's Careers in Movies

There was a time when women were limited as to which jobs they would find. Costume design was considered a woman's area as well as hair and make-up. But today you will find them working along side or in front of men in most movie careers.

# Women as Producers

Some of the top box office hits as well as the Oscar winning best picture for 2005 were produced in full or in part by women. Dreamworks' *Match Point*, Focus Features' *Brokeback Mountain*, Lions Gates' *Crash*, and Sony's *Memoirs of a Geisha* all had women as producers, those with the ultimate responsibility for completion of the movie. **Lynda Obst**, successful since the Dawn Steel era, has always held that being on set each day is the most important part of a producer's job during the production phase of a movie. Those are the times when little things can grow into big headaches quickly when a producer isn't available with a plan B to handle a production problem. While she has produced such box office hits as *Sleepless in Seattle* and *How to Lose a Guy in 10 Days*, she felt her arrival in Hollywood coincided with the dawn of a new era. She says, "there was one 'girl' at every meeting to read scripts, write notes, and dispense mineral water. The people doing this job, the first non-clerical one widely open to women, have come to be known as 'd' girls, short for development girls."[3]

**Laura Ziskin**, while working on her third *Spider-Man* movie, was sought after on the set by its star, Toby McGuire, as often as he looked for the director. After previous successes, Ziskin wanted a challenge. So, she asked the studio to give her the "biggest mother" they had ready for production. That was the first *Spider-Man* movie and she was so successful at bringing in nearly a half-billion dollars on the sequel that she completed the third version which premiered last summer.

# Women as Directors

Women directors became more notable and began being considered successful directors at the helm of films when those films grossed over $100 million dollars in the last decade.

From 1990 to 2000 several women directors were at the helm of films that grossed over $100 million dollars:

| | |
|---|---|
| Nora Ephron | $115.7 million for *You've Got Mail* in 1998 |
| Betty Thomas | $144.2 million for *Private Parts* in 1998 |
| Penelope Spheeris | $121.6 million for *Wayne's World* in 1992 |
| Nancy Meyers | $182.8 million for *What Women Want* in 2000 |
| Mimi Leder | $140.5 million for *Deep Impact* in 1998 |
| Penny Marshall | $107.4 million for *A League of Their Own* in 1992 |

Earnings for directors and producers vary widely; usually what they earn per film is based on a percentage of what a film grosses (earnings before costs come out). With that in mind, Laura Ziskin should have received a respectable sum for her production of Spider-Man 2 which grossed nearly three quarters of a billion dollars worldwide, keeping her salary equal to men for producing, but women do not direct enough films to keep up on the director side.

# Women Working Below-the-Line

While working in post-production (or any other below-the-line position) was not previously on the top of the list of successful careers for women, many of today's sought after techies are making up to five-figure salaries per week. Proving themselves first helped get them hired in lead post-production positions. **Caroline Ross**, editor of New Line's epic fantasy feature *Dungeons & Dragons,* paid her dues as first assistant editor on *Terminator 2* and *Judgment Day,*[4] *an*d as co-editor on *Starship Troopers* before she was allowed to take the lead. Steven Spielberg counted on his editor, Verna Fields, when cutting *Jaws*. He suggested a contest where each of them would stop the movieola (a viewing device) on a frame they felt was the right place to cut. If they both stopped on the same frame, they knew it was right and the cut was made. He said, "everyone called her 'Mother Cutter' because she was so earthy and very maternal. She did her editing at her pool house in the San Fernando Valley. It was a very Amish kind of workplace."[5] Quentin Tarantino knew he wanted to work with a female editor on *Pulp Fiction,* someone who would nurture him through the process. **Sally Menke**, filled that editing position and worked with him on *Reservoir Dogs* as well.[6]

**Tina Hirsch,** the first woman to head up the American Cinema Editors (the A.C.E. appears after their names on the credit role), feels the reason editing was the first profession in which women really made their mark was because it isn't a physical job. She says; "It's not like you're carrying around big cameras or sound equipment or standing there holding a boom."[7]

Cinematographer, **Ellen Kuras,** got her feet wet while working for director Spike Lee. Working closely with Lee on *Son of Sam* (1977), Kuras represented an emerging trend in the industry in which many male A-list directors hired women in key below-the-line positions according to a December 2000 article in *The Hollywood Reporter.*[8]

Costume designer, **Edith Head**, (1897-1981) had always been the woman to emulate if you wanted a career in the wardrobe field. From her first designs during the silent era to her last picture *Dead Men Don't Wear Plaid*, she has always been thought of in Hollywood as *the* costume designer. She received the last of eight Oscar's for dressing Robert Redford in *The Sting.*[9] The latest Oscar winner for Best Costume Design was Elizabeth Byrne.

If fashion is your dream, designing is not your only option. Movie studios have wardrobe departments that house not only seamstresses who complete the designs, but also shoppers. This new career has garnered much attention as young women are found in department stores and boutiques looking for that "just right" article of clothing for the star that wasn't available on the many racks hanging in the wardrobe warehouse on the lot.

# Spotlight

JoAnn Perritano has been the Unit Production Manager on such films as The Red Dragon, Rush Hour 2, Rush Hour 3, Van Helsing and The Prophecy. This is how she got started.

*It all started on a trip to California when I was in the 6th grade. While visiting Universal Studios, I turned to my Aunt and said, "people do this for a living?" I was bitten by the Hollywood bug.*

*During my college years at Emerson, my love for the entertainment industry grew. Between my Junior and Senior year, I landed an internship in Hollywood with Entertainment Tonight. I arrived in LA not knowing a sole. I rented an old Jalopy from a company called Ugly Duckling and shared a dorm room at USC with a couple of pre-med students attending summer school. I got everything out of my summer in Hollywood that I could. Working for E.T. was an unbelievable experience. Following the internship, I returned to Boston to finish my senior year.*

*In late April, Entertainment Tonight came calling. Someone was headed out on maternity leave. I was about to graduate college and I had my first offer for a paying job in Hollywood—even if it was only for 3 months! I bought a car and my best friend (Zucco) and I made our way across the country to start our new lives. My three month stint at Entertainment Tonight quickly turned into three years. While I was there, I visited many film sets. I realized that making movies was a part of the business I wanted to explore. The problem was, I had no film experience and no film contacts. I took a huge risk. I left my paying job at Entertainment Tonight with the goal of making movies. I once again turned to an internship. I went knocking on the door at Roger Corman Studios. I worked on 2 films while I was there—for no money. I struggled to pay the rent and put food in my stomach, but I was having a blast and learning so much.*

> *Through a friend, I got my first paying job on a feature film—the classic "Maniac Cop 3"! That led to a long relationship with a company called NEO Motion Pictures. They gave me some incredible opportunities including a chance to be a Unit Production Manager on a film called "American Yakuza" starring a then unknown Viggo Mortensen.*
>
> *I just celebrated my twentieth year in the business. I am currently Co-Producer/Unit Production Manager on Paramount Pictures "G.I. Joe".*

## How to Get Started in Movie Careers

The best way to get started in any of the entertainment fields is through an internship. Some women will do multiple internships to eliminate areas and hone in on others. If you are currently a college student, pursue as many internships as allowed by your academic program. If an internship is not possible, there are several training programs in the movie industry that are available. The Directors Guild of America (DGA) training program is offered each year to those interested in becoming production managers and beyond. An exam is given in several cities followed by interviews by panels and then a final interview in Los Angeles. These two year paid programs offer the trainee experience in both film and television shows on the lot and in the field. Casting agencies also have training programs where many notable professionals today got their start. The most famous is the William Morris Agency training program. Information about all of these training programs can be found on the internet. Entry level positions as "assistant to" producers and studio executives will give you an opportunity see how all the movers and shakers deal with the day to day happenings in the movie industry. Set PA's and office PA's (Production Assistants) are the most common entry-level positions when one is interested in working on a film. Set PA's often are called Runners because they are asked to run (or drive) scripts to actors all over Hollywood.

## Minority Women and the Movies

In 1954, Dorothy Dandridge became the first African American woman nominated for an Academy Award for Best Actress in *Carmen Jones*.

While she didn't receive the Oscar, it did put her on the map. It also afforded her the starring role five years later in *Porgy and Bess* (1959). "Prejudice is such a waste," Dandridge once concluded. "It makes you logy and half-alive. It gives you nothing. It takes away." She believed, "If I were white, I could capture the world."[10]

There have been some significant changes for African American women in U. S. films since 1990. Actors such as Whoopi Goldberg have chalked[11] up 90 credits for either voice-overs, movies or television appearances since 1990; Oprah Winfrey besides being producer and executive producer of 12 features, has appeared in 10 movies, she has made countless appearances, archival footage, and TV guest appearances; Whitney Houston is involved as producer and executive producer in several films, has starred in notables such as, *Waiting to Exhale, The Bodyguard,* and *The Preacher's Wife,* and won countless singing awards; and Halle Berry continues to find leading roles after winning her Oscar in 2002 for *Monster's Ball.*

Salma Hayek is becoming known for her body of work according to *Time Magazine*'s August 22, 2005 issue highlighting the 25 most influential Hispanics in America. Her first notable role was in the 1995 film *Desperado.* But, she entered the big time when she produced and starred in *Frida,* which was nominated for six academy awards. Working with her director, Julie Taymor, she was encouraged to do her own singing, and she obliged.[12]

When Queen Latifah received her Golden Globe for *Chicago,* her career options doubled and she went from being a supporting actress to command the leading role in her 2006 release *Last Holiday.*

According to the 2005 Hollywood Writers report executive summary, women and minorities represent more than 50 percent and 30 percent respectively of the U.S. population, and, yet, women writers represent only 18 percent of the total while all minority groups combined account for a mere 6 percent.[13]

## Movies and the Glass Ceiling

The Directors Guild of America's 2005-2006 Women Members Contact List shows there are 1,293 women available to direct features, but female directors are certainly among the minority when it comes to the top grossing film directors in Hollywood.

From February 1 to March 5, 2006 a billboard at Sunset and Cahuenga in Hollywood displayed the concerns of more than "the Guerrilla Girls" and "Movies by Women." The headline read "Unchain the Women Directors." It also revealed that only 7 percent of the top 200 films of 2005 were directed by women. Additionally, no woman director had ever won an Oscar and only three had been nominated. The two groups behind the campaign wanted to know why women heading the studios weren't doing more for women and minorities. They encouraged those women heading studios to "open up that boys' club and hire more women and people of color. It worked in medicine, business and law. It worked in the art world. Now it's Hollywood's turn. Rattle that cage, break those chains! LET WOMEN DIRECT."[14]

They were "directing" their challenge to a few. However, those few had broken through the glass ceiling that all women in Hollywood wanted to break through. Until the end of 2005, Sherry Lansing's name was synonymous with "Hollywood studio mogul." Her position as CEO of Paramount Studios brought women entering the industry lots of hope. If she could break into this male-dominated arena from her high school teaching position by reading scripts at night for $5 an hour, they could find their path to success in the industry. When she announced her retirement, many women were concerned that women leaders of major motion picture studios might be just a fluke. But today, Stacey Snider, as Co-Chairman and CEO of Dreamworks, and Amy Pascal as Chairman of Sony Pictures Entertainment Motion Picture Group, are proving that fear wrong. Other women on that ladder are Gail Berman, President of Paramount Pictures, Paula Wagner, CEO of United Artists, and Elizabeth Gabler, President of Fox 2000 Pictures.

The pioneer for these women was Dawn Steel who made history as the first woman to run a major motion picture studio. As President of Columbia Pictures she oversaw an annual combined production and marketing budget of more than $400 million. She was sometimes referred to as "steely Dawn" because of her attempt to be "one of the boys." In her autobiography *They Can Kill You But They Can't Eat You,* she revealed her theory about rising to success. She used the "Jeffrey Katzenberg Theory of Getting Things Done. Which is this: *If they throw you out the front door you go in the back door, and if they throw you out the back door you go in the window, and if they throw you out the window you go in the basement. And you don't ever take it personally.*[15]

According to a recent report from Women in Film, 21 percent of the films released in 2004 employed no women directors, executive producers, producers, writers, cinematographers, or editors. Not a single film failed to employ a man in at least one of these roles. They also found that by genre, women were most likely to work on romantic comedies and romantic dramas and least likely to work on horror and action adventure features. Women comprised 31% of individuals working on romantic dramas, followed by 30% on romantic comedies, 22% of documentaries, 17% on dramas, 16% on comedy/dramas and 16% on sci-fi features, 15% on animated features, 14% on comedies, 9% on action adventure features, and 4% on horror features.[16]

In the Lauzen study for 2004, she found that only 5% of directors are in the top 250 films in 2004, representing a decline of 6 percentage points since 2000 when women accounted for 11% of all directors.[17]

According to the *New York Times,* "four of the six major studios have women in the top creative decision-making roles" and "some now see Hollywood as a gender-balanced model for the rest of corporate America. Women have come to predominate in Hollywood at a time when less than one percent of Chief Executive offices in the fortune 500 are female, and none of the nation's top 100 publicly held companies have a female chief."[18]

While there are women in leading positions, and there are more women working in this industry, there still seems to be a problem with breaking that glass ceiling for some categories of employment. The one concern, which seems most obvious to even the lay-person whose only connection to films is watching them in theaters, is the director. It is also an area that is of great concern to women in Hollywood. The Alliance of Women Directors (AWD) hosted a panel discussion on the past, present and future employment opportunities for women directors in Hollywood. Successful women directors sat on the panel and the consensus was that women "have to have that inner strength and toughness."[19] They also felt that "In an industry that is very competitive, women who have finished films should be commended for their ruthlessness. You're committed, you're single-minded, you are not indecisive, you know what you want, and you will not be distracted from that."

In the January/February, 2006 issue of *Mother Jones,* Clara Jeffery notes that actors over the age of 40 account for 30% of the movie roles, while actresses over the age of 40 account for only 9%.[20]

This is obviously a gap that needs fixing. More female students are enrolling in film and television schools than in the past. Entry level positions are open to both men and women in Hollywood as runners, set PA's, and Assistants to executives. As women climb the ladder there are more women who are mentoring their sisters. Women in Film and Video as well as several other groups established for women in this field, are meeting regularly to see how they can increase the numbers of women rising to those decision-making positions. If only they could figure out the director problem.

## Diversified Diva: Shirley MacLaine

From her first Academy Award nomination for her role as Ginny Moorhead in *SomeCame Running* (1958), to her current role as Miss Ellie Ewing in *Dallas* scheduled to be released in 2007, Shirley MacLaine's movie roles number more than fifty, and in four of them she sang. She received the Oscar for *Terms of Endearment* after twenty years in the business.

She also received a Golden Globe for her 1988 role in *Madame Sousatzka.*

Her credits as a producer and a writer cover both film and television, and she directed the Academy Award nominated documentary, *The Other Half of the Sky: A China Memoir* (1975) and *Bruno* (2000.) In addition, she appeared as herself on television ninety-three times. Her qualification as a multimedia diva includes her work as an author of several books beginning with *Out On A Limb,* followed by *The Camino* (2001), and *Out On A Leash* (2003.) She is working on a new book with the working title "Saging (sage-ing) and Aging."

Born Shirley McLean Beaty, (named after Shirley Temple) she changed her name to Shirley MacLaine when a Broadway producer continued to find it difficult to pronounce Beaty.

Her brother Warren didn't seem to encounter the same producers. Her legs have always brought her recognition, maybe because she was a notable dancer.

During the late 1980's, she led a series of weekend-long "Higher Self Seminars," teaching people about her views on many aspects of New Age practices and techniques.

More recently she created her own website, shirleymaclaine.com and has her own radio shows, *The Encounter Board,* and *Independent Expression.*

She married Steve Parker in 1954 and they divorced in 1982. They have one child, Sache Parker.

# Summary

While many felt the DVD industry would wipe out the movie industry as we know it, there are still cineplexes being built all over the country. Today many of you are watching these movies on your cell phones or other newly designed devices, the making of such entertainment is still thriving in Hollywood. So no matter how you choose to enjoy them, women will still be needed to create them.

In this chapter we have pointed out that the major studios are controlled by larger entities and the top rung of those ladders are held by white men, again.

Additionally, we pointed out that while females struggle to get involved at the very top levels of movie-making, some of the best films have been produced and/or directed by women—*Brokeback Mountain, Crash, Memoirs of a Geisha.* Women persevere behind-the-sets as editors, cinematographers, costumer designers, etc.

We hope you have learned that the glass ceiling for women is firmly in place, especially again for minority women, a phenomenon that the FCC keeps promising to do something about. As yet, the movies are still a white domain, which means the system is pretty narrow if not closed altogether to some.

Table 6.1 Major Motion Picture Studios

| Sony Pictures Entertainment | Disney Enterprises, Inc. | New Line Cinema Corporation | Paramount Pictures* | Time Warner | Twentieth-Century Fox |
|---|---|---|---|---|---|
| (www.sonypictures.com) owns Columbia Pictures, Screen Gems, TriStar Pictures and part of MGM | www.corporate.disney.go.com | (www.newline.com) owned by Time Warner (www.timewarner.com) that also owns Turner Broadcasting, AOL, Home Box Office and Time Inc. and Warner Bros. Studios | is owned by Viacom, (www.viacom.com) CEO and Chairman Philippe Dauman; Sumner Redstone is Executive and Chairman of the Board and Founder | (See New Line Cinema) | is owned by News Corp (www.newscorp.com) that also owns Fox Television Studios, Blue Sky Studios and Fox Searchlight Pictures |
| CEO & Chairman of the Board Michael Layton | CEO & President, Robert A. Iger | Co-CEO & Co-Chairman: Robert K. Shaye & Michael Lynne; Toby Emmerich is Pres., New Line Productions | CEO & Chairman of Paramount's Motion Picture Group: Brad Grey* | CEO & Chairman of Board, Richard D. Parsons | CEO & Chairman of Fox Film and Entertaiment: Bill Mechanic; President of Twentieth-Century Fox is Mark Kaner |
| Total Executives (Sr. Mgmnt Team): 4 | Total Executives: 17 | Total Executives (New Line only): 8 | Total Executives (Viacom): 15 | Total Executives: 9 | Total Executives: 13 |

*Table 6.1 Major Motion Picture Studios (continued)*

| | | | | | |
|---|---|---|---|---|---|
| Females: 1 | Female Executives: 3 | Female Executives: 1 | Female Executives: 3 | Female Executives: 2 | Female Executives: 1 |
| Total on Board (Sony Corp.): 15 | Total on Board: 12 | Total on Board (Time Warner): 11 | Total on Board: 12 | Total on Board: 11 | Total on Board: 13 |
| Total Females on Board: 0 | Total Females on Board: 3 | Total Females on Board: 2 | Total Females on Board: 2 | Total Females on Board: 2 | Total Females on Board: 0 |
| Woman with highest clout position at SPE: Amy Pascal, Co-Chairman of SPE | Woman with highest clout position: Christine M. McCarthy, Exec. VP, Corporate Finance and Real Estate and Treasurer | Woman with highest clout position (New Line): Camela Galano, President, New Line International Releasing, Inc. | Woman with highest clout position: Shared between Judy McGrath, MTVNetworks, Chair & CEO; and Debra Lee, BET, Pres. & CEO | | Woman with highest clout position: Anthea Disney, Exec. VP, Content |

*Could not locate detailed analysis of Paramount Motion Pictures Group.

*Table 6.2 Percentages of Women as Directors, Writers, Executive Directors, Producers, Editors and Cinematographers*

| Year | Men | Women |
|------|-----|-------|
| 2004 | 84% | 16% |
| 2003 | 83% | 17% |
| 2002 | 83% | 17% |
| 2001 | 81% | 19% |
| 2000 | 83% | 17% |
| 1999 | 85% | 15% |
| 1998 | 83% | 17% |

# Notes

1. www.imdb.com.

2. This is from the website of Women In Film, a non-profit organization, and the findings of a study completed by Martha Lauzen, San Diego State University called, "The Celluloid Ceiling: Behind-the-Scenes Employment of Women in the Top 250 Films of 2004," published at www.wif.org.

3. *Hello, He Lied* by Lynda Obst, Broadway Books, 1996.

4. *What Do Editors Do?* BBC (2005).

5. Ibid.

6. Ibid.

7. *Hollywood Reporter*, December 2000, Gina McIntyre, "Pair of Aces."

8. *Hollywood Reporter*, December 2000, Women in Entertainment special issue, "Women to Watch."

9. www.imdb.com.

10. *Hollywood's All-Time Greatest Stars*, Andrew J. Rausch, Citadel Press (2003).

11. www.directmag.com/mag/marketing_actors_actresses (Copyright 2005 Primedia Business Magazines and Media.

12. Luscombe, Belinda (2005). "The Hollywood Dynamo." *Time* Magazine. August 22.

13. www.wga.org.

14. www.guerrillagirls.com, 2/27/06.

15. *They Can Kill You, But They Can't Eat You,* Dawn Steel.

16. www.wif.org.

17. Martha Lauzen's 2005 Celluloid Ceiling Report.

18. http://www.nytimes.com/2005/04/24hass.html.

19. AWD, 2005.

20. Jeffrey, Clara (2006). "Limited Ambitions." *Mother Jones*, January/ February.

# Chapter Seven

## Turning the Radio Down a Little

Volume is relative. Each generation has distinct radio listening habits that include how loud the volume should be. Turning it down is also relative.

> *FYI—My (Carole's) experience with hands-on radio has been in writing and recording commercials and public service announcements for the Boston market. During my years at WBZ television I often got asked to come into the (radio) booth to talk about what was happening on the show I was working on. Larry Glick was noted for dragging us on air during his overnight shows if we were walking down the hall to get a candy bar to give us energy during our late night edit sessions. There were also the times when we would provide the radio side with copy of what we were planning for the nightly news stories.*
>
> *FYI—My (Lee's) experience with radio was a volunteer reader for radio for the blind back in the 1990s. I used to read the newspaper via WASU-FM out of Augusta, Georgia.*

### Major Radio Outlets

There are thousands of commercial radio stations across the country, as well as NPR (National Public Radio) and nearly as many networks that provide news, sports, talk and great music. Westwood One claims to be the largest provider of audio content in America. Internet radio stations are most popular on college campuses, giving students an opportunity to shine with a captive audience. Satellite radio has become the newest endeavor in the competition, but will listeners pay for such information?

## Who Owns Radio?

According to StopBigMedia.com, the top three companies owning large groups of radio stations are Clear Channel with 1194 stations in the U.S., Cumulus with 313 stations and Walt Disney with 227 radio stations. Citadel Broadcasting is not far behind with 223 stations. These owners acquire, merge and sell stations quite often, which could account for the fact that Journalism.org lists Citadel Broadcasting in third place as can be seen in Table 7.1.

## The Music Industry

By the end of the 1950's radio dramas became too costly and money was filtered into television instead. Then, radio broadcasting changed dramatically with the onslaught of "rock 'n' roll" (or rock and roll). Many would agree that rock 'n' roll saved radio. Halper writes: "In 1954, a new style of pop music that the young people liked was making its presence felt. Originally descending from so-called race music, or rhythm and blues, it came to be known in the early 1950s as rock 'n' roll."[1]

The recording industry revolutionized radio in another way also. Women's programs on radio were no longer popular. Radio stations could make more money from sponsors with Top 40 formats and purchasing records was not necessary since record companies sent free records to stations daily. This allowed for women to reach fame as recording artists, like the Andrews Sisters, who aired for the first time in 1945. It also allowed women recording artists to be known solely by their first names, like Barbra, Cher and Madonna, who still count on the radio today to bring in the audiences for their live concerts.

Disc jockeys, mostly male, were ensconced in a scandal in the early 1960s for accepting bribe money to play certain records. Eventually, radio stations got competition from one innovative young man at the time that somehow got sponsorship to host an afternoon dance show for teens called, *American Bandstand*. The host, Dick Clark, today, is still known as America's youngest teenager, and is watched each December 31st as he rings in the New Year.

Meanwhile, women withdrew again to backstage in radio, owning and operating stations, producing shows, and marketing programs. While they were also struggling in the new venue of television to be on-the-air hosts, news announcing for women on both radio and new television was still almost unheard of. As television moved in, many women, thinking perhaps the hills were greener on the other side, moved slowly out of radio and into the new medium.

Lisa Phillips, a former radio reporter and news director of KTPR in Fort Dodge, IA, feels that "We are turning to radio for stories, for music, for community, for insight, for laughter, the kinds of things that brought families around the Philco in the days before television took center stage in the living room."[2]

# Careers in Radio

Many of the careers or occupations noted here are for both radio and television, so in the television chapter, there may appear to be repetition. The BLS Occupational Outlook for the Radio and Music Industry list the following job descriptions:

- **Program Directors**—The directors are in charge of on-air programming in radio stations. Program directors decide what type of music will be played, supervise on-air personnel, and often select the specific songs and the order in which they will be played. Considerable experience, usually as a disc jockey, is required, as well as a thorough knowledge of music.
- **Announcers**—Most radio programming today consists of very few news items; National Public Radio however continues to have strong support for news and information programs, so there is opportunity for announcers in radio still. On popular music stations, announcers are called disc jockeys, who play recorded music, may do a bit of news and provide other community information as well as radio commercials. The BLS reports that technological advances have simplified the monitoring and adjusting of the transmitter, leaving disc jockeys responsible for most of the tasks associated with keeping a station on the air. Traditional tapes and CDs are used only as backups in case of a computer failure. Announcers and

disc jockeys need a good speaking voice; the latter also need a significant knowledge of music.

- **Technical occupations**—Employees in these occupations operate and maintain the electronic equipment that records and transmits radio or television programs. The titles of some of these occupations use the terms ,audio engineer, technician, and operator, interchangeably.
- **Radio operators**—They manage equipment that regulates the signal strength, clarity, and range of sounds and colors (keeping the meter under the red area) of broadcasts. They also monitor and log outgoing signals and operate transmitters.
- **Audio technicians**—They work within the stations to regulate the volume and sound of all broadcast.
- **Broadcast technicians**—These technicians set up and maintain equipment, even portable transmitting equipment and they might maintain the stationary towers for the station.
- **Master control engineers**—They make sure that all radio station program elements, on-location feeds, pre-recorded segments and commercials are transmitted without problems and according to Federal Communications Commission requirements.
- **Network and computer systems administrators and network systems and data communications analysts**—They are responsible for the design, set up, and maintenance of all systems of computer servers. These servers store recorded programs, advertisements, and news clips.

# Women's Careers in Radio

In the early days of broadcasting, female commentators were limited to "women shows" that normally aired in the midmorning to early afternoon. During the early years, Mary Margaret McBride, "The First Lady of Radio," presided over a daytime radio talk show that achieved enormous popularity. Her show usually included fifteen minutes of homemaking tips and a half-hour interview with guests from fan dancer Sally Rand to comedian Jimmy Durante, as well as Eleanor Roosevelt, President Harry S. Truman, and Queen Elizabeth II. She eventually was named "the most important woman in the United States" by the United Nations and thousands of fans attended a spectacular tribute to her in Madison Square Garden in New York City.

Kay Morton also did a popular chat show for women on KXOK in St. Louis. Another show produced to boost the morale of servicemen was *Reveille with Beverly* in 1942. A favorite daytime serial was *Aunt Jenny's Real Life Stories*, airing Monday through Friday at 11:45 am. Each week a complete story was presented in five episodes, the leading character played by Edith Spencer. Each Tuesday evening at 9 pm, women would enjoy the writings of Madelyn Pugh while listening to *I Love Lucy,* played of course, by Lucille Ball. It was the sequel to a successful run from 1948-1951 of *My Favorite Husband* which she played opposite Richard Denning.

Soap Operas made most women gather around the radio. One of the longest running soap operas (1936-1956) was *Ma Perkins* played by Virginia Payne. Another popular soap from that era (1936-1952) was *Big Sister* starring Alice Frost as Ruth Evans. She portrayed a modern-day heroine who gave up her life and love to take care of her orphaned siblings. However, *Stella Dallas* is considered by many as the mother of all soap operas. The leading role was played by Barbara Stanwyck as early as 1937. Popular until its departure in 1955, it was one of the most enduring daytime drama series on radio. In 1990, Bette Midler starred as *Stella* on the big screen. Eventually, once more and more people acquired TV sets, soap operas on radio met their demise and resurfaced on television, e.g., *All the Days of Our Lives* and *General Hospital* were on radio beginning in the late 1930s.

The *Helen Hayes Theater* was a weekly dramatic anthology that was on the air at various times from 1935 until 1946; and, The *Hedda Hopper Show*, loaded with gossip from her newspaper column, ran from 1930 to 1950 on CBS. Every weekday at 12 pm from 1938 to 1951, you could turn on *High Noon* and hear, "It's high noon in New York and time for Kate Smith."

One of a few women, Margaret Arlen, remained an announcer after the war and continued to get respectable ratings on women's shows where her forte was finding interesting people to interview. Another woman, Lucille Small, at WWRL in New York City, found to her surprise that the program director wanted her to stay but not as an announcer. She was offered the position of disc jockey of a new hit record show aimed at teens.[3]

Positions like this for women in radio were unheard of and few and far between at best. Meanwhile, women held onto farm broadcasting jobs, which meant that they did shows about agriculture and techniques for raising healthier animals. Donna Halper points out that one exception to the rule for women occurred when Frieda Hennock joined the Federal Communications Commission in 1948, the first woman ever to be appointed. Male journalists who interviewed her regarding the appointment were quick to write that she was attractive, glamorous, blonde, and a smart dresser. Fortunately, Hennock became a "tireless advocate for educational radio and TV."[4] Another expert in educational programming was Judith Waller, who began her career as station manager of WKGE in Chicago. Her expertise in educational programming led her to write numerous articles about how radio could be a valuable asset to education. She won a "Golden Mike" award in 1954. One of the first documentary award winners was Edith Meserand, a founding member of American Women, who began her career as a station manager. She also spent several years in news and special features at WKOR radio.

Virginia Graham began her career on radio in the early 1950's, and became one of radio's great talk show hosts. At that same time, women station owners were being noticed. The first woman to own a radio station was Marie Zimmerman. Not far behind, Gene (short for Imogene) Burke of KRUX in Phoenix was just another of 25 women who ran their own stations. Other notable women owners were Dorothy Stimson Bullitt of KING AM & FM who purchased it in 1947 and turned it into King Broadcasting in Seattle; and Lady Bird Johnson, who owned KTBC in Austin, Texas.

Today, one woman who seems to supply the music as well as family values, is **Delilah**. Her nationally syndicated show can be heard each night for three hours on 218 stations. She was only in the seventh grade when she taped her weekly school news and sports show, *Delilah, on the Warpath*. Her listening audience has followed her life from her anchor position in Boston, to her current busy life in Seattle, through her adoption and birthing of several children and the renovation of her beloved homestead, "The Farm."

**Dr. Laura** (Schlessinger), considered the most influential female radio talk show host since the 1990's, thinks people also turn to the radio for advice. Her daily three hour program aired from coast to coast, has resulted in her authorship of eight New York Times best sellers and four children's books. As the first woman to win the Marconi Award for Network/Syndication Personality of the Year, she parlayed her notoriety into a one-woman two-act show called *Dr. Laura: In My Never To Be Humble Opinion*. Not all of her listeners find her advice and opinions positive. The advice-dispensing physiologist angered the gay community when she called homosexuals "deviant" and homosexuality a "biological error." The *Stop Dr. Laura* website, received over 50 million hits and 3 million visitors. Over 170 advertisers abandoned her television show causing it to be cancelled on March 30, 2001.

**Barbara Carlson**, morning shock jock and political commentator on Minneapolis' KSTP-AM, and former Governor's wife, takes an entirely different approach. She discusses real-life dilemmas using her own life trials for examples.[5] Her autobiography details enough challenges in her life to keep her on the air into the next century.

In April 2000, WNYC Radio, Oregon Public Broadcasting premiered *Satellite Sisters*. **Julie, Liz, Sheila, Monica and Lian** are five real sisters who grew up in a large family and share that wisdom each week on air. They developed a radio program that discusses "the practical nuts-and-bolts choices about everything from career moves to childcare issues, from writing a will to what to serve at Thanksgiving."[6]

Another notable WNYC radio personality is **Brooke Gladstone**, who was National Public Radio's first media correspondent. The former print journalist is currently the co-host and managing editor of *On the Media*.

# Spotlight

Donna Halper was the first woman announcer at Northeastern University and then spent more than two decades in broadcasting as a respected media historian, management consultant and book author.

*When I was growing up, AM top-40 radio was king. I had several favorite disc jockeys and wanted to be like them. It never occurred to me that women weren't allowed to be top 40 jocks; I just assumed none had applied, and I was eager to change that. When I got to Northeastern University in Boston, I immediately went to my college station, but to my surprise, they told me I couldn't be on the air because I was "a girl." It would take me 4 years to persuade a program director to give me a chance, but in October 1968, I became the first woman in Northeastern's history to be on the air, and from there I became the first woman everywhere I worked.*

# How to Get Started in Radio Careers

Many college students intern at radio stations in their market ripping scripts, researching stories and cataloging 30 second spots. The latest craze for student interns is on the promotion side of musical groups who are traveling around the country appearing at night club venues. These students help with the design of posters and work the shows when the acts appear. If there was a radio station on their college campus, many students had their own shows introducing "musical selections" and reading commercial copy.

# Minority Women in Radio Careers

The RTNDA/BallState University Annual Survey reported in 2004, and we find an 11.8 percent minority radio workforce in radio but once again, we don't know the real numbers for minority women.

If we rely on the Bureau of Labor Statistics (BLS) data for end of year 2005, all we get is a total number of 64,000 minority women who work in "radio and television broadcasting and cable" but this does not help us much with respect to radio alone.

The Maynard Institute that tracks diversity reported in 2005 that the RTNDA/Ball State University annual survey found that the percentage in minorities in radio dropped from 11.8 percent last year (2003,since the survey was for 2004) to 7.9 percent. Yet, radio stations (low power, high power, AM, FM and satellite) are increasing. And, today there are 650 Hispanic radio stations in the U.S. and Puerto Rico.[7]

The BLS for 2004 reported that in the category of musicians, singers and related workers, 36.4 percent were women, of which 8.6 percent were Black/African American women.

African Americans have struggled doubly hard for their own shows throughout the post-war years; inevitably, southern stations refused to air anything about race or the race struggle, even if products were targeted for black clientele in the commercials. The first radio stations to devote entire formats to black-oriented programming were owned and operated by white entrepreneurs who tailored radio shows and advertisements solely for African Americans. The inequity continued for the next 15 years until the country was entrenched in a battle for civil rights.

Academy Award winning actress, for her performance as Mammy in *Gone With the Wind,* Hattie McDaniel was among the few black radio performers to find success. Her radio role was that of Beulah on *Show-*

*boat* and she was a regular on shows like the *Billie Burke Show* and *Blueberry Hill.*

While black women were already working in suburban black radio stations prior to the 1960s, few persevered long enough to survive all the racial strife. One female did though. Trudy Haynes who had been an announcer at a black radio station prior to both the fight for civil rights and the FCC ruling about equal opportunity in 1970,[8] made it to KYW-TV in Philadelphia where she did both news and human-interest stories, much like Carole Simpson who had also started out as a radio news reporter. Today Simpson is a news anchor for *World News Tonight Sunday.*

Wendy Williams, referred to as both the "Queen of Urban Radio," and the "biggest mouth in New York," would certainly defy a hold on minority women in radio today. Her daily afternoon drive show on WBLS allows her to give advice and disarm celebrities into revealing their secrets. In her market, LITE-FM is usually the number one show during the afternoon drive, and Wendy's show is number two.[9] Her mentor was another black woman in radio, Carol Ford. Wendy recalls, "I was a Carol Ford wanna-be. That was the person I looked up to, whose career path I wanted to take. I remember when Carol Ford came to New York doing afternoons on KISS-FM, they brought her in with billboard ads and subway ads. She was a black woman with her own show and she was very well paid. They even put her up in a fancy hotel. She came into New York diva style."[10] Today, other black women are looking to Wendy as someone to replace. Wendy thinks it takes futuristic vision.

One successful entrepreneur is Cathy Liggins Hughes who established an African-American-owned broadcast conglomerate, Radio One. The 66-station-chain is the dominant influence in at least 13 of the 22 cities in which Radio One operates and is valued at $2 billion. She employs not one newsperson at her four Washington DC stations, something that Mark Lloyd criticizes. "Ownership is clearly not enough in a market culture that puts profit over every consideration. But ownership particularly over television, is a start."[11]

# Radio and the Glass Ceiling

If we look at table 7.1, there are 48 officers and members of the board, out of which only 11 are women (or 24%). It is almost another closed system. Today, nearly 90 percent of radio program directors are men, according to a recent study by the trade group Mentoring and Inspiring

Women in Radio (MIW), only 10.7 percent of the 10,634 stations listed in the M Street Publications database in late 2004 showed women programmers. In the top 100 markets, women produced only 8.9 percent of the programs heard on radio. Women were 30 percent of the sales management positions at 10,451 stations, but 10 years ago, there were only 2 percent of women sales managers at radio stations.

If minority-owned radio stations, like those of Hughes mentioned above do not employ minority newscasters or any news announcers whatsoever, and if instead we have radio stations that simply rotate music round and round, what kind of a culture will develop? Add to that question, if in radio news, we do have more minority voices, how much will it add to our diverse culture?

In spite of it all, some women not only succeed in radio, they jump into other media genres and succeed again and again. Our next diversified diva is an example of what we mean.

## Diversified Diva: Cokie Roberts

While many might think of Cokie Roberts as a television personality, her career in radio spans more than three decades. From her first National Public Radio (NPR) job covering politics on Capital Hill, through her rise in television every Monday on *Morning Edition,* to her current title of Senior News Analyst, she has continued to think of radio as the best way to reach people. In her book, *Public Radio: Behind the Voices,* Lisa Phillips says that Cokie told her she kept the radio gig so long because she felt a sense of connection with her listeners. "If you want to reach people in government, people in the Fortune 500, people in academia, in the journalistic community, and then, remarkably unlike any other mainstream news organization, younger people, because it's on many college campuses, NPR is the place to do it, and you can do it with some depth and some humor."[12]

In her book, *We Are Our Mothers' Daughters,* she refers many times to how her women friends sustained her. It might have been because she shared a small cubicle with Nina Totenberg and Linda Wertheimer at NPR. Or, it might just be that the three of them along with their husbands have a standing Saturday night dinner date. But, of these Three Musketeers, Cokie Roberts stands out in our minds as a multimedia Diva.

In addition to her radio career, she worked in television, first as a producer of a quiz show for teens, then as a host on a roundtable-style program for journalists, and then as a reporter in Greece for magazines, CBS radio and television. She was the first regular female panelist on *This Week with David Brinkley* and when he left, she co-hosted the show with Sam Donaldson for ABC from 1996 to 2002. She not only won an Emmy and the Edward R. Murrow Award, but she was the first journalist to win the prestigious Everett McKinley Dirksen Award for coverage of congress.

To fill out our multimedia requirement (three different mediums), she writes a weekly syndicated column and she added book authoring to her resume. In addition to the aforementioned best seller, she also wrote *Founding Mothers: The Women Who Raised Our Nation* (2004); and, with her husband Steven, *From This Day Forward* (2000).

This former president of the Radio and Television Correspondents Association is the daughter of congressman Hale Boggs and after his death in a fatal plane crash, was referred to as the daughter of congresswoman Boggs, as her mother filled that role for several years. A breast cancer survivor, she and her husband have a daughter, Rebecca and a son, Lee. They also have four grandchildren.

# Summary

Women announcers, show hosts and interviewers were a needed commodity during WWII. When the men came home, women in radio were either relegated to jobs in the back of the station or in some cases managed to leap over to the new mass medium called television and there carve out careers. Some careers made it, some were short-lived. Soap operas on radio remained popular even after they were also broadcast on television because the gap between the television haves and have-nots took years to close, especially in rural areas. By the mid-1950s, however, 75 percent of all households in major American cities had a television. Meanwhile, music literally saved radio; rock 'n' roll brought on a whole new meaning for the small portable box; record companies thrived and so did disk jockeys. For some reason, male DJs were the norm and everyone, including women, helplessly accepted it.

The FCC formed in 1948 and the first woman on the commission was appointed; at the same time a female station manager in Chicago, not the norm, won a Golden Mike award in 1954. Another woman purchased a radio station and soon 25 women were running their own stations, one was Lady Bird Johnson, wife of later President Johnson.

Meanwhile, DJs suffered a scandal with something called payola, accepting bribes to play certain songs. Still, rock 'n' roll was here to stay as Dick Clark and the *American Bandstand* took off.

The outlook today for women in radio is much brighter, with sixteen females serving as General Managers of public radio stations across the country. Women like Laura Walker at WNYC in New York, Jane Christo at WBUR in Boston and Ruth Seymour of who turned around KCRW from a little under-performer into one of the most listened to radio stations in Los Angeles.

*Table 7.1 Three Top Radio Companies*

| Broadcasting Company | President or Chief Executive of Company | Number of Corporate Officers | Number of Board Members | Women Executives or Directors | Who owns it? | CEO of Parent Company |
|---|---|---|---|---|---|---|
| Clear Channel | Lowry Mays, Chairman and CEO | 25 | unknown | 9 | Lowry Mays (may have a partner) | N/A |
| Cumulus Media Inc. | Lewis W.Dickey Jr., Chairman, President and CEO | 5 | 5 | 0 | This is a public company | N/A |
| Citadel Broadcasting Corp. | Farid Suleman, Chairman and CeO | 4 | 9 | 2 | Forstmann Little & Co., a Wall Street leveraged buyout firm; it is a public company | N/A |
| TOTALS | | 34 | 14 | 11 | | |

# Notes

1. Halper, p. 169.
2. Phillips, Lisa A. (2006). *Public Radio: Behind the Voice*. New York: CDS Books.
3. Halper, p. 136.
4. Halper, p. 137.
5. Carlson, Barbara with Jess Cagle (1996), *This Broad's Life*,. New York: Pocket Books.
6. Dolan, Julie, Liz Dolan, Sheila Dolan, Monica Dolan, and Lian Dolan (2001). Satellite Sisters' Uncommon Senses. Seattle,Wa: Riverhead Books.
7. Arbitron, 2003.
8. According to Barry D. Umansky, a regulatory reviewer of the FCC, the requirements of written equal employment opportunity programs were to be written out by broadcasters in 1970. Stations that did not employ women and minorities at certain minimum percentages of their local workforce received an in-depth review of their EEO programs at license renewal time. (www.tvtechnolog.com) February 5, 2003.
9. Williams, Wendy (2003). *Wendy's Got The Heat*. New York City: Atria Books.
10. Ibid.
11. Lloyd, Mark (2005). "Remove the Barriers to Minorities in Media." American Progress Organization, August 10. (www.americanprogress.org/site/pp.asp?c=biJRJ80VF&b=959321).
12. Phillips, Lisa A. (2006). *Public Radio: Behind the Voice*. New York: CDS Books.

# Chapter Eight

# Mirroring the Image of TV

There is an argument among scholars and media owners about whether television mirrors society or whether society mirrors television. If you believe in the latter, this means people are walking robots and merely follow a television culture. If you believe in the former, this means you are more optimistic in the belief of individualism.

> *FYI—I (Carole) began my television career as an intern at WBZ-TV in Boston. I was there only two weeks when we experienced the famous Blizzard of '78. I went to the station on Monday and couldn't leave until Friday. Because most of the producers didn't make it to the station that afternoon I found myself learning very fast how to produce a newscast. When they asked me to "go get the network feed", I thought it meant "call the caterer." I learned the ropes very fast and decided before I went home on Friday that I wanted to become a television producer.*

Many people believe that being "on television" is greater than—well than anything. Career seekers, therefore, are abundant. For a female or male to make it into network television or show hosting takes years of moving around the country being seen in various television markets. Many don't make it, yet the opportunities remain.

Nielsen Media Research reports the television penetration of U.S. households went from 9.0% in 1950 to 98.2% today.[1] Accordingly, the number of television networks went from three at its premier to six broad-

cast networks (with the merging of CBS' UPN and Warner Brothers WB
to the new CW, it dropped to five commercial networks); with the introduction of cable allowing the viewer of the small screen over 100 cable
channel options today.

# Major Television Outlets

The National Broadcasting Company (NBC) was the first television network to begin regular television programming. It launched at the 1939
World's Fair in New York, but its first regular prime time series did not
air until 1944. The American Broadcasting Company (ABC) and the
Columbia Broadcasting System (CBS) joined the daily schedule in 1948.
While the Dumont Network was the actual first licensed American network, established by the Allen Dumont Laboratories, it went off the air
in 1955. In 1969, Public Broadcasting System (PBS) joined the airways
with news, documentaries and educational programming
     In the 1990s three broadcast networks joined the prime time lineup.
The FOX Broadcasting Company, launched in 1993; The Warner Bros.
Television Network (WB) founded in 1995; and, the United Paramount
Network (UPN), also launched in 1995. In 2006, UPN and WB merged
to become the CW Network. Today, with the explosion of cable television, you can choose to view programs on more than 100 channels targeting specific areas of interest. Cable networks are more targeted to
specific demographics, like the Food Network, Home & Garden Network, Black Entertainment Television, DIY Network for do-it-yourselfers,
and Spike TV geared toward men.

# Who Owns Television Networks?

ABC is owned by Disney, CBS and the CW are owned by Viacom, NBC
is owned by GE, and FOX is owned by News Corp. PBS is a non-profit
corporation whose members are America's public television stations.

### The Language of Television Programming

When we examine the programming offered on television and the women
who influence those shows, we need to break down the day into industry
language. Television programming is separated by genres such as, News,
Talk Shows, Sitcoms, Dramas (sometimes referred to as Episodics), Soap
Operas and Reality Shows. Each of the genres we examine falls into one

of the following categories: daytime, prime-time, early fringe or late night. News programming is offered throughout the day and is sprinkled on talk shows like *Meet the Press* or *Face the Nation*, and news magazine offerings like *Dateline NBC, 20/20* or *60 Minutes*.

# Careers in Television

In each of the genres mentioned above there are directors, producers, writers, talent/actors and a multitude of below-the-line positions. Above all of these are the station and network management and owners. While television has many of the same career descriptions as film in chapter 6, some positions are unique to television.

- **Showrunners**—These are sometimes referred to as Executive Producers. They are responsible for each week's episode of their comedy or drama for the season.
- **Associate Producers**—They are usually given a segment of a show to research, write and produce. They also oversee the editing process.
- **Unit Managers**—They are responsible for the budget in their departments, newsrooms or stations.
- **Crew Chief**—This person is in charge of all the technical employees in the newsroom and will usually be the one to go into the field to scout out remote sites to make sure a live shot can be sent back to the station from each location.

# Women's Careers in Television

Women have held higher-level positions in cable programming longer than in the other TV sectors. Lifetime has a majority of women at the top and Oxygen not only has women executives at the top, but produces programming especially for women.

While women have been a major target audience category since the 1950's, very few women were originally involved in deciding what content would be broadcast. Anne Nelson, the longest employed female at CBS remembers sitting in meetings as the only female when she was responsible for the business affairs of the early vaudeville acts turned television stars. Being "one of the boys" felt natural to her then and it rings true when she says that none of the "suits" thought of her as a woman. In her current position as Vice President of Business Affairs for

Entertainment, she says that women vice-presidents proliferated in past decades only because it was a way to make it look like they were doing something for the women. Today she encourages her granddaughter Skye to go after her dream of working in television because times have changed and what happened to her would never happen today.[2]

Female role models for students wanting to work in the television entertainment industry today are in abundance. Not only do we have women serving in decision-making roles like Anne Sweeney, President of Disney—ABC Television Group; Nancy Tellem, President of CBS Paramount Network Television Entertainment Group; Judy McGrath, Chairman and CEO, MTV Networks; Dawn Ostroff, President of Entertainment, the CW; and Geraldine Laybourne, Chairman and CEO of Oxygen Media; but, women are serving on the executive decision making level in surprising numbers. These women did not have role models and many of them are pioneers for female students today.

Carole Black, former President and CEO of Lifetime Entertainment Services, says she was influenced most by her Armenian grandmother, who raised her after her parents' divorce. She taught her that you always have to give back. Today, after a career promoting such programs as *Strong Women* and *The Division,* she remains committed to educating women on major issues, on-screen and off. She spent 11 years as a full-time mother and tells women they can have it all, just not at the same time.[3]

Nancy Tellem, President of CBS Paramount Network Television Entertainment Group worked under male mentor, Les Moonves, and came up through the business affairs ranks rather than the creative side. She was named the fifth most powerful woman in the entertainment industry by the *Hollywood Reporter* in December, 2006. The number two most powerful woman in their issue was Anne Sweeney, President of Disney's ABC Television Group. She is also a believer in women being able to have it all, and even though she continued to climb the ladder in her career while raising her children, she cautions women to accept the fact that some days will be more difficult than others.[4]

As one of Oxygen's founders, Geraldine Laybourne, has led the company to be a strong advocate for women. Oxygen's mission is: Intelligent entertainment for women and the men who love them. But, the night before she held her first executive meeting, she asked her husband to help prepare her by learning sports facts like innings were in baseball, goals were in hockey, periods in basketball and quarters were in football. The first topic came up and she made a reference to a tennis term that was really used in a different sport and her male supervisor told her "You don't have to be one of the guys. That's not why you're here. You're here because of who you are."[5]

In the 2005 fall season, prime-time programming was staffed with over one hundred creative decision-making women. What do we mean by creative decision makers? The writing staff, the producing staff and the directing staff all are responsible for the creative side of programming. There are increasing numbers of women also serving in the technical side in positions on camera, in control rooms and in post-production. There have always been more opportunities for women in casting and today that fact remains.

## News

When students look at careers in broadcast news there are a number of role models to study; Barbara Walters, Andrea Mitchell, Cokie Roberts, Soledad O'Brian, Campbell Brown, Diane Sawyer and the first female nightly news anchor, Katie Couric to name a few. Jessica Savitch rose to substitute anchor for the prized Nightly News, but whether she would have sat in the chair as the regular anchor will never be known because her life was cut short in 1983 with her tragic death at the age of 36.[6] Campbell Brown filled in when Brian Williams was on assignment or vacation. She also co-hosted *Weekend Today* and was lined up to replace Katie Couric when she became the first permanent woman *Nightly News* anchor at CBS. But the NBC executives decided Meredith Viera from the *View* would be their new co-anchor on *Today*. Campbell Brown can now be seen regularly on CNN. Lesley Stahl has been a reporter for CBS News for more than 30 years. She was White House correspondent for the CBS Evening News during the Carter, Reagan, and Bush administrations; the host of *Face the Nation* from 1983 to 1991; and has been a correspondent for *60 Minutes* for the last 14 years.

Andrea Mitchell, NBC's Chief Foreign Correspondent continues to be seen on regular news programs throughout the week even as some would fear her age would become a detriment.

Unlike their male counterparts, women find more difficulty remaining on camera as they mature. In 2002, when Greta Van Susteren was hired away from CNN, her facelift, *blepharoplasty* and dental implants gained media attention for a media pundit with a reputation as being somewhat plain, a rarity in U.S. television broadcasting. While it is universally known that women need to be younger looking and more attractive than their male counterparts, the only woman who has been quoted on the topic is Barbara Walters who concludes; "Women in television don't get older, they just get blonder."[7]

In 1984 the President of NBC, Larry Grossman, put two women in charge of a new type of news program. It was to be called *Summer Sunday* and would be produced by Karen Curry from *Today* and Cheryl Gould from *Overnight*. The show was also staffed mostly by women and would be anchored by two women, Linda Ellerbee and Andrea Mitchell. But, without long-term money budgeted, the program was doomed to failure. Ellerbee devoted a chapter to the misplaced and under-budgeted program in her 1986 account of witty news stories *And So It Goes.*[8]

Most of these women in news work behind the scenes as well as on camera, either as a producer, executive producer or writer. It's very common in broadcast news for reporters or anchors to also be involved in writing or producing. Martha Roundtree was co-creator of the NBC News program, *Meet the Press*, as well as the first moderator. She remains the only female moderator in the show's history. However, it is physically impossible to report or anchor/moderate and also direct a newscast. One position is in front of the camera and the other is behind the camera, and the jobs are completed simultaneously.

## Talk Shows

From Virginia Graham to Ellen DeGeneres, talk show hosts have been involved with the content of their shows on a daily basis. In retrospect, over the last three decades it seems like talk shows were being hosted by every woman who could talk. Daily shows were hosted by Sally Jesse Raphael, Ricki Lake, Jenny Jones, Gabrielle Carteris, Carnie Wilson, Barbara DeAngelis, Dr. Laura, Rosie O'Donnell, Whoopi Goldberg, and Dr. Ruth.

While Barbara Walters accepted the Emmy for Outstanding Talk Show for the *View* in 2003, Ellen has taken home that honor since. Both women serve as executive producers of their shows. In fact, most talk shows are staffed with a majority of women on the creative side. It makes sense that daytime talk shows would play to more women than men, and topics that would be of interest to women would more easily be conceived by women.

Late night talk shows have greater appeal to men. And yet, Ellen Brown, a skilled music and cable variety show director, has been directing Jay Leno on the *Tonight Show* since his first substitute appearance in 1992. And, Liz Plonka has been directing *Late Night* with Conan O'Brien since 1995.

Joan Rivers has been the only woman to host a late night talk show, after appearing as guest host for nearly three years. She thinks women still have a long road to travel before cracking that slot. In her words: "We may be out of the jungle, but we're still fighting over the one banana."[9]

Melissa Young, former *Tonight Show* music producer, feels women are still subject to harassment on the job. Her experience during an awards show production taught her that developing a thick skin is a woman's greatest defense. While she felt management was not as supportive as she would have liked, success is her greatest response. Today, she has left the *Tonight Show* to pursue freelance producing to slow down on her former daily demands and devote more time for marriage and a family.[10]

## Sitcoms

*I Love Lucy* is considered to be the first successful sitcom on television starring a woman. While Lucille Ball was instrumental in not only the on-camera work, but also the creative process, Madeline Pugh-Davis is the unsung hero. As one of the original writers, she guided the storylines and dialogue that was so vital to its success. Charlotte Brown was another pioneer who wrote and produced *The Mary Tyler Moore Show.*

Yvette Lee Bowser has been a sitcom producer for 14 years. After creating *Living Single* in 1993 for FOX, and producing it for five years, she created *For Your Love* in 1998 for NBC. She came up with the idea for the show from conversations she held with her husband in her bathroom. She enjoys getting up close and personal with her actors, but feels a heavy responsibility each week in getting the show in the can. She finds it appropriate and endearing when they call her "mother" on the set.[11]

Amy Sherman-Palladino was credited as the vision behind the *Gilmore Girls,* which received accolades for its content and style. As co-executive producer with her husband John, she was responsible for the look as well as the content of each episode. Lesli Linka Glatter directed the show's original pilot and was stunned by the intelligence of the dialogue in that opening script.[12] Patricia Palmer, line producer, compares Amy's style to that of Norman Lear's. The show won numerous awards and after completing 100 episodes on UPN, went into syndication.

## Dramas

Sometimes referred to as episodics, dramatic programs have more women in responsible positions today than in any other genre. With more women working in the creative roles of producer, director or writer, the female touch has been as much a part of storylines as that of their male counterparts. CSI's Carol Mendelson has been called the brains behind the success of Jerry Bruckheimer's number one drama series. She is involved with every episode from first draft through post-production. Jennifer Love Hewitt is a producer on her CBS drama *Ghost Whisperers* lending her expertise in developing her character, which shows both courage and compassion.

Barbara Hall creates shows she wants to see, and while she has created two shows with strong central female characters who appeal to women, she wasn't targeting a female audience when she came up with *Joan of Arcadia* or *Judging Amy*.[13]

Most women rise through the ranks to produce dramatic series. Serving first as production assistants and then spending time as associate producers. Being organized and always having a plan B will help them rise faster.

## Soap Operas

Women have always been associated with the soap opera genre. Not just as the primary viewers who will buy advertisers' products, but as a career for women writers. Stories are drawn from pop culture as well as public affairs issues in order to keep the genre fresh and entertaining as well as current.

When we watch awards shows and read the trades, Agnes Nixon is often termed the "queen" of contemporary soap opera. While she did create *One Life to Live* in 1968 and *All My Children* in 1970, it is Irna Phillips who is responsible for the daytime drama as we know it today.[14] Not only did she create the longest running soap, *The Guiding Light,* which premiered in 1952, but she also created *As the World Turns* in 1956*, Another World* in 1964, and *Days of Our Lives* in 1965.

Today there are teams of women writers on soap opera staffs and female students around the country who compete for the internship opportunities and entry level positions as writers' assistants in order to break into the soap opera genre.

## Reality Programs

Since the threat of the writer's strike in 2003 hit the entertainment industry, Reality Programming has multiplied ten fold. Even though that strike never came to pass, reality programming continued to rise. And, during the actual writers strike in 2007, networks scrambled to add even more to their lineup. In the beginning of reality programming as we know it today *Real World* was already a success with a teenage demographic on MTV, *Big Brother* and *Survivor* were just making the scene. Then reality television programming went wild. From *The Littlest Groom* to *Who Wants to Marry My Dad*, the networks were tripping over themselves in a race to find the next *Joe Millionaire*. The FOX network made its mark when that show's finale brought a greater rating than the Super Bowl. New staff categories have surfaced with this genre—stunt producers, background checkers and superdome casting sessions. *American Idol* has over 30 million viewers casting their votes each week to eliminate one of the final contestants.

Reality programming continues to thrive.

---

# Spotlight

Sue Ann Staake-Wayne is the Director on Face the Nation, seen on Sunday mornings on CBS. She also has her own production company SAS Productions out of Herndon, Virginia. This is how she got started.

*I majored in Radio and Television at the University of Maryland, and when I graduated I found a job in the Traffic Department at Channel 5 in Washington, DC. I figured it was a way to get my foot in the door. After two years a job became available in the Promotions Department producing spots. Because I was already in the building and had gotten a reputation as a hard worker, I got the promotion. I was on my way.*

# How to Get Started in Television Careers

Again, there is no better way to get started than with an internship. Newsrooms will use production assistants to rip scripts, log tapes and run errands. The track in news if you want to be a producer is to start as a production assistant, then an associate producer and finally a producer. If you want to direct the news you need to move from a production assistant to an assistant director or stage manager and finally director. Directors must join the DGA (Directors Guild of America), but producers are not part of a union. They have a guild and after qualifying can become a member of the Producers Guild.

# Minority Women and Television

Two notable women in news stand out today. Belva Davis became the first black woman television reporter on the west coast at a CBS affiliate in San Francisco. Connie Chung was the first Asian American woman reporter, the first Asian American woman anchor in Los Angeles, and the first Asian American woman to co-anchor a network news program. Only the second woman in 17 years to co-anchor an evening news program (Barbara Walters was the first) Chung is the only regular woman staffer at all three leading news networks with ABC's 20/20, the NBC Nightly News and the CBS Evening News with Dan Rather. Colleagues at CBS called it the "Connie Broadcasting Service."[15] She then moved to CNN and after a few years at home raising her son, she was seen co-hosting with her husband Maury Povich *Weekends with Maury and Connie* on MSNBC.

According to DGA News, nearly 40% of the top forty series hired no women directors in the 2003-04 season. Fifteen of the top-40 shows didn't hire women directors, minority directors, and six excluded both women and minority directors. Despite minimal gains over the last few years, women television writers have yet to surpass the twenty-something percent share they have traditionally claimed.[16]

Mara Brock Akil, showrunner for *Girlfriends* says "It isn't automatic like it might be for a white man running a show, but being a woman talking about women's issues on *Girlfriends* has absolutely helped me with credibility. Now that I've been running the show for three seasons, it's not as much of an issue."[17]

Sarah Finny Johnson, showrunner on the former UPN's *The Parkers* believes "until there are as many women in positions of power in television as there are men" she has a responsibility to help other women make it onto the playing field.[18]

Eunetta T. Boone, showrunner on the former UPN comedy, *One on One*, feels that "men have a certain dialogue and shorthand with each other that women in this job have to learn".[19]

But, the most notable rise of an African American woman in the television industry today is that of Shondra Rhimes who created and executive produced the 2005-2006 season's number one medical drama, *Grey's Anatomy* for ABC. She's not sure her gender or skin color change the way her superiors treat her. "When things are going well, my race and gender aren't a factor. When they go poorly, I think they're pointed to as a possible reason for failure" she says.[20]

## Television and the Glass Ceiling

Sue Ann Staake-Wayne, a director on *Face the Nation*, decided early on to give up the pursuit of being "talent" and to use her creativity behind the camera. She knew her gender played a part in station decisions even before someone from WTTG-TV in Washington, D.C. told her she was hired in the promotions department because she was a woman.[21] Additionally, she knows she has been refused jobs because of her gender. In other words, she is quite aware of the metaphorical glass ceiling. When she got her first directing job, she purposely lowered her voice an octave and still speaks in that tone. She also will never wear perfume in the control room. Even though she feels that women have to be better in order to get and keep the job, she reports that on *Face the Nation,* the whole back deck (the associate producer, producer, executive producer) are women and the only male in the control room is the technical director. She will not believe the glass ceiling has been cracked in local broadcast news, however, until women are hired in greater numbers above the position of Bureau Chief which she feels is as far as they let women rise.

Her feelings are confirmed by the National Association of Broadcasters who report that of the 1600 television stations in the U.S., only 132 of the general managers are women.

When it comes to primetime network series the news is good. According to the Hollywood Reporter's Women in Entertainment, December 2006 article on Boss Ladies, creating and running primetime shows is almost a gender-neutral pursuit. Showrunners Kari Lizer of *The New Adventures of Old Christine*, Katie Jacobs of *House*, Shondra Rhimes of *Grey's Anatomy*, and Meredith Stiehm of *Cold Case,* are proving that true. They feel that running shows has for the most part removed the gender issue from the equation.[22]

So the network television medium is shattering that glass ceiling. And with Oprah Winfrey premiering her new network in 2008 (OWN) the corporate owners issue will be cracked.

# Diversified Divas: Mary-Kate and Ashley Olsen

As we look at women in television who have succeeded in more than two mediums, we would be remiss if we didn't choose the youngest self-made millionaires before they were ten years old as our multimedia television divas.

These fraternal twins, Mary-Kate and Ashley Olsen, began their television careers at the age of nine months in the role of Michelle Tanner on *Full House,* and held that role for nearly a decade. They became the youngest producers in history when they teamed up with Robert Thorne to form Dualstar Entertainment Group.

In addition to record albums, music videos, and three full-feature movies, they created their own video service called The Adventures of Mary-Kate and Ashley, which produced a multitude of adventure videos for tween viewers. Since *Full House* went off the air (it can be seen daily in syndication) the twins have put out 169 books, have a bi-monthly magazine titled after them, and their clothing and cosmetic lines can be purchased in Wal-Mart and Claire's. Their recent license agreement with the Sprouse brothers (also twins) allows the brothers to launch a quarterly magazine patterned after their own.

VH1 ranked them #3 on their list of "100 Greatest Kid Stars," the Hollywood Reporter named them the "Most Powerful Young Women in Hollywood," and rumor has it they are worth about 100 million.

They have an older brother, Trent, and a younger sister, Lizzie (Elizabeth.) Both Mary-Kate and Ashley attended New York University where Mary-Kate majored in Photography, and Ashley majored in Psychology.

They have drawn much publicity in the last few years, both for their weight loss and their love lives. In February of 2005, Mary-Kate filed a $20 million dollar libel suit against the *National Inquirer* for alleging her involvement in a drug scandal.[23]

# Summary

Since the first show aired at the World's Fair in New York, women have been working behind and in front of the camera on television.

Marlee Matlin convinced producers that characters could also be deaf and got her first television role on *Reasonable Doubts*. She has continued to grace the small screen with guest appearances on prime-time series like the *West Wing* and her new weekly competition on *Dancing with the Stars*. But her greatest contribution to television was when she lobbied congress to pass a law allowing a little chip in television sets which resulted in closed caption viewing.

The role of being a successful television executive and mother has been a concern for some because of the long hours required in television production. But, Kate Sedrowski took on that research in her senior year at Emerson College. After interviewing more than fifty women working in Hollywood at all levels of entertainment, she found that most of them felt you could have it all, just not at the same time.

One of Hollywood's most powerful woman in entertainment, Anne Sweeney, President, Disney-ABC Television Group, probably responded to the concerns of all women entering the television arena, either in front of the camera or behind, when she said "it's sad that any woman would feel they had to displace their desire to have a personal life in order to have a career. You just have to rely on your ability to be a problem solver and no one ever expects you to have all of the answers all of the time."[24]

The television career for women outlook is bright. As evidenced by the partial listing below in Table 8.1, women are holding CEO and Chairmanship positions in all divisions within the world of entertainment. And, while station managers positions are still difficult for women to obtain, network corporate ownership has been cracked by Oprah Winfrey.

## Table 8.1 Female Presidents, Chairmen and CEO's in Television

| | |
|---|---|
| Angela Bromstad | President, NBC Universal Television Studio |
| Betty Cohen | President and CEO, Lifetime Entertainment Services |
| Susanne Daniels | President of Entertainment, Lifetime Entertainment Services |
| Bonnie Hammer | President, USA Network and SCI FI Channel |
| Paula Kerger | President and CEO, PBS |
| Geraldine Laybourne | Chairman and CEO, Oxygen Media |
| Debra Lee | Chairman and CEO, BET |
| Janice Marinelli | President, Buena Vista Television |
| Judy McGrath | Chairman and CEO, MTV Networks |
| Sheila Nevins | President, HBO Documentary and Family |
| Christina Norman | President, MTV |
| Dawn Ostroff | President of Entertainment, The CW |
| Abbe Raven | President and CEO, A&E Television Networks |
| Robin Schwartz | President, Regency Television |
| Angela Shapiro-Mathes | President, Fox TV Studios |
| Carolyn Strauss | President, HBO Entertainment |
| Anne Sweeney | President, Disney-ABC Television |
| Nina Tassler | President, CBS Entertainment |
| Nancy Tellem | President, CBS Paramount Network Television Entertainment Group |
| Dana Walden | President, 20th Century Fox Television |
| Laurie Younger | President, Buena Vista Worldwide Television |
| Lauren Zalaznick | President, Bravo |
| Cyma Zarghami | President, Nickelodeon |

# Notes

1. Nielson Media Research Report, January 2005.

2. Personal Interview with Anne Nelson, December 2005.

3. *Variety*, January 24, 2005, supplement.

4. "Because I Am a Woman," documentary by Kate Sedrowski.

5. Ibid.

6. Blair, Gwenda, *Almost Golden*. Avon Books, p. 344.

7. "10 Questions for Andrea Mitchell," by Barbara Kivat, *Time*, August 22, 2005.

8. Ellerbee, Linda, "And So It Goes" Berkeley, p. 216.

9. *Still Talking*, Joan Rivers w/ Richard Maryman, Random House, 1991, p. 142.

10. "Because I Am a Woman," documentary by Kate Sedrowski.

11. "What Is a Producer," E Entertainment Network, 2003.

12. *Hollywood Reporter*, Gilmore Girls, 2004.

13. "Crusader for Girl Warriors," *Television Week*, Leslie Ryan, 11/10/2003.

14. Museum of Broadcast Communications archives.

15. www.museum.tv.

16. Women Writers' Share of Employment, 1998-2004.

17. "Women Who Run the Show," Mollie Gregory, St. Martin's Griffin, 2002.

18. Ibid.

19. Ibid.

20. Ibid.

21. Personal Interview, August 2005.

22. *The Hollywood Reporter*, Dec. 2006, "Boss Ladies," by Ray Richmond.

23. www.tv.com.

24. "Because I Am a Woman," documentary by Kate Sedrowski.

# Chapter Nine

---

# The Fast Pace of Cyberspace:
# The Internet

*FYI—Both Lee and Carole can remember their first internet experience (Lee: I remember the old dial-up; the computer was connected to the telephone line and a coded number was activated. It seems like this happened a hundred years ago. The internet provided email ability and I was so thrilled at the idea that a message could somehow travel through the air. I believe the first search engine I used was called Lycos. I remember having many problems with dial-up—circuits would get busy or you would be tying up your own phone line. In all, I remember a lot of frustration during the early days of internet (1994-2000)— seems like a century ago). (Carole: My first real experience with the internet was when my husband and I tried to design and program a website for our company, caughtontape.biz (Caught on Tape Productions). Because it has a lot of video segments we wanted something that would show them on the largest screen. Bluevoda was the answer for us because their viewing window is larger than most. We use a Mac however and they service PCs so they had a lot of trouble with the site. It was a real ordeal and we finally had to agree to let people enter the site and then choose which format to view before they could see any video).*

This chapter is about women and the internet, and like the other chapters, we outline careers, the status of women in these careers and the giants of the industry and where women fit in their corporate structures and boards.

We do not concern ourselves in this chapter with the status of the hardware giants, like IBM, Dell, Hewlett Packard, Compaq, etc. We realize there must be a computer available to connect to the internet. Therefore, we'll focus on computer programming and web design for internet. Added note: we are not suggesting that one needs to get a degree in computer programming to write or update web pages for companies because that skill can be easily taught. We only suggest that if web page creation and design is a goal, computer program language will have to be learned somewhere.

Infoplease, a data site, reports that there were 1 Billion internet users worldwide and in 2006, there were 208 Million Americans.[1] In a December 2005 report by the Pew Research Center, more men than women use the internet. Women use email more robustly—spend more time in email topics with friends. Both men and women use the internet equally for online transactions. Lastly, men are more likely than women to gather material for hobbies, participate in sports fantasy leagues, download music and videos and listen to radio via the internet. Not a surprise, men are more interested than women in technology.[2]

What is a surprise almost daily is the usage of the internet. We're sure you know what a blog is and are quite familiar with MySpace and Facebook. Do you know what a vlog is? It's a blog with video. And, we're sure you have heard of YouTube, Innertube, Revver and iTunes. While YouTube permits you to upload your own videos, Innertube owned by CBS allows you to download popular television series such as CSI. There's also Revver, a video sharing network and of course iTunes software that permits downloading from the internet music, videos, TV shows and podcasts. This, we predict, is only the beginning. Eventually, we will be able to download shows on television and movies for theaters *sooner* than they hit either the television screen or the movie theater. That is the daily surprise about the internet.

## The History of the Internet

According to the Internet Society, the internet's history is like this:

- J.C.R. Licklider of MIT August 1962 discusses Galactic Network concept—everyone quickly accesses data and programs from any site.

- Leonard Kleinrock of MIT publishes first book on subject of packet switching theory in 1964.
- G. Roberts connects the TX-2 computer in Massachusetts to the Q-32 in California with a low speed dial-up telephone line; in 1966 Roberts puts together his plan for the ARPANET.
- By the end of 1969 four host computers are connected together into the initial ARPANET and the internet's birth was assured.[3]

# Living Without the Internet

Much of cyberspace information is created by specialists in marketing, advertising and public relations on behalf of clients. It is a fact that the World Wide Web is an open marketplace. Today, it seems odd if a company does not have a WEB site with its own domain name. On a global basis, women in other countries probably know more about American women than American women do about them, but that gap is narrowing. The internet as a medium of mass communication, where information can be accessed within seconds, is improving the world for women. Women are getting connected via cyberspace networks, and while only 60 percent of American families may have computers, and only 50 percent are connected to the internet, the fact is that the WEB is helping people get together.[4]

Cyberspace dating is a reality today. Couples interact via email or even via web-cameras, the need for private space is not an issue because each is secure in his or her own desk-space. On a real date, each would be worried about moving too close to each other the first time they meet. We probably all know couples that met via cyberspace, then met in person, dated and married.

Now, with the amount of "blogging" found on the internet, even if someone is not net-dating, sometimes relationships can develop over blogs—opinions about life that include topics A through Z. Some people even post their photographs with their blogs or will include a video-clip. A website called cyberjournalists claims that there are 50 million blogs, and 175,000 new weblogs are created each day. Many blogs are linked to media, the website claims, and sites that are the most-linked to from blogs lists the *New York Times* as number one.[5]

For women, especially rural women in remote areas of the country who do have a computer and some WEB access, the internet is doing for them what radio women-hosted shows did for women in the 1920s and 1930s—allowing women to learn about other women. The problem is that while the internet is attractive to women, basically the computer is not. Nevertheless, as Media Report to Women reports, computer usage is pretty evenly divided between men and women:

> Males and females have had approximately equal rate of computer use since 1997. In 1997, males were more likely than females to be internet users. Since August 2000, males and females have had virtually identical rates of internet use (U.S. National Telecommunications and Information Administration).[6]

## The Internet as a Mass Medium

Vault, an online career organization, explains the terms **internet** and **World Wide Web**. They both mean the same thing, they write—"an interrelated set of documents, files and data joined together by hyperlinks." And they note, the internet is everywhere, practically, now that 70 percent of Americans, or 203.5 million people were regular internet users in 2005 and spending more than $22 billion in e-commerce sales.[7] Because the internet can reach mass audiences at all times, and because news and entertainment is a large part of the material conveyed to mass audiences, the internet fits within the parameters of a mass medium.

## Uses of the Internet

Americans definitely are big consumers of the internet evidenced by giants like Amazon.com and eBay.com as well as by the fact that most companies have web pages because they know consumers are looking for their companies. Young female college students it is reported are 51% more likely to buy online than their male peers.[8]

Other uses include email, research for information, entertainment and chat rooms.

The word, "natter," means "have a chat." Chat rooms could easily then be called Natter rooms and such rooms are open to anyone. Chatting across the globe for women, especially in third world countries when there is a computer and internet available, has brought women closer together, into a type of global village that Marshall McLuhan[9] envisioned television's impact would have.

Marketing of products [similar to television commercials] is now a norm; information inquiries are made easier via library, university, mass media outlets, and government connections. It is the newest of the mass media and the most persuasive of them all.

## The Language of the Internet

Let's define some terms[10] we hear all the time in our daily interactions with the internet:

- **Blog**—an online journal posted by people about themselves in the public cyberspace area.
- **Browser**—A program that allows users to view web pages. AOL's Netscape Navigator, Apple's Safari, and Microsoft's Internet Explorer are examples.
- **Cyberspace**—Refers to all the computer networks on the Internet and distinguishes the physical world from the virtual world.
- **Internet**—Began in 1989 and is a network of millions of computers from all over the world. The internet allows computers to trade information using telephone lines, fiber-optic cables and satellite links. It is also called "the Net."
- **Internet Service Provider**—The company that provides access to the internet usually a local cable or direct satellite company, for its customers, e.g., Comcast.net, Time Warner cable, HTC, etc.
- **Network**—A network is created when computers are connected allowing people to share information. The Internet is an example of a large network.
- **Search engine**—A program that searches for information on the WEB by looking for specific keywords and returns a list of information found on that topic. Ask Jeeves for Kids is a search engine. So is Google, and now there is Ask.com.
- **URL**—Stands for Uniform Resource Locator which is the specific location or address of material on the internet. For example, the URL for one of the writer's web pages is http://www.leebollinger.com

- **Web Site**—The URL gets us to a website which is a collection of pages linked together.
- **WWW**—World Wide Web is an infinite number of games, web sites, pictures, sounds, stories and other things all connected to each other through links on the Internet.
- **Web**—In Answers.com found by using the Google search engine, the word "web" has a literal meaning and is not an acronym. It derives from the woven fabric definition and came about in the early days of dial-up to get connected to "a web of telephone wires."

## Who owns Internet Browsers, Search Engines and Computers?

Most people know that **Microsoft** is a giant in the software industry, but it also owns a browser, **Explorer** and according to an article in USA today has a roughly 95 percent market share[11] and a search engine, **MSN.** They create programs for computers and programs for the internet, or world wide web to use for a fee. Their Microsoft Office software has become available for MacIntosh (owned by **Apple**) users without the separate modem requirement. Apple's CEO and original owner, Steve Jobs, cofounder in 1976, battled with Bill Gates for years about access to Microsoft software (such as Microsoft Office). Jobs is also co-founder and CEO of Pixar Animation Studios (1986) that created such animated films as *Toy Story, A Bug's Life, Monsters, Inc., Finding Nemo* and *The Incredibles.* Pixar merged with the Walt Disney Company in 2006, and Jobs now serves on their board of directors as well. **Microsoft's** stock listed at $27.96 per share on March 14, 2008 with a market cap of $259.85 Billion. Its products include browser Explorer, MSN search engine, Hot Mail, Xbox video game system, Windows Mobile software for mobile devices, Office Outlook, Office Communicator, new versions of Windows XP and Media Centers and tablet PCs. Hot Mail had 250 million active accounts at the time of their 2005 Annual Report Letter to Shareholders.[12]

**Apple's** stock listed at $126.61 per share on March 14, 2008 with a market cap of $107.88 Billion.[13] Unlike Microsoft, Apple has found a niche in hardware, software and what we call "gadgets." Some of their products include: hardware: eMac, iMac, MacBook, MacMini; software: AirPort Express, AirPort Extreme, Aperture, Apple Remote Desktop,

Final Cut Express HD, iLife, iTunes, iWork, Motion, Mac OSX, and others; gadgets: iPod, iPodHi-Fi, iPod and others. Apple also owns **Safari**, an internet service provider and with it an email extension.

These two companies and a few others are the current giants in software (and in the case of hardware, Apple's MacIntosh) and the internet service.

**AOL now Time Warner**'s stock listed at $ 14.03 on March 14, 2008 with a market cap of $55.1 Billion. (We talked about Time Warner in previous chapter). In its subidiary, AOL's portfolio we find the following: AOL.com subscription service to 10 million members in U.S at end of 2007, as well as the browser, **Netscape**, and MapQuest, Moviefone, AOLCityguide, AOLshopping, CompuServe, AOL Phoneline, AOL Family Library, AOLMobile, AOL Music Now, educational software, and others. Its email service, AOL.com reportedly has 150 monthly page views and 109 million visitors each month to its web properties.

**Google.com** is the most interesting search engine, co-founded in 1998 by Larry Page and Sergey Brin with now 5,000 employees worldwide. The most recent stock share price for Google was $437.92/share March 14, 2008 and had a market cap of $129 Billion.

**Yahoo.com** is a search service engine, like Google, its biggest competitor. The company was co-founded in 1994 by Ph.D.s out of Stanford University, David Filo and Jerry Yang, and has become the world's largest global online network of integrated services, according to its web page, company overview.[14] Its March 14, 2008 closing stock price was $26.71/share and a market cap of $129.4 Billion. Here is a paragraph from its 2005 Annual Report that discloses much about the giants on the internet:

We face significant competition from companies, principally **AOL, Google**, and **Microsoft**, that have aggregated a variety of Internet products, services and content in a manner similar to **Yahoo!**. **AOL** has access to content from Time Warner's movies, television, music, book, periodical, news, sports and other media holdings; access to a network cable and other broadband users and delivery technologies; and considerable resources for future growth and expansion. **Google**, in addition to an Internet search service, offers many services that directly compete with our services, including a consumer email service, desktop search, local search, instant messaging, photos, maps, shopping services and advertising solutions. **Microsoft** has introduced its own Internet search service and has announced plans to develop both paid search and features that may make Internet searching capabilities a more integrated part of its Windows operating system.[15] (See Table 9.1.)

# Careers and the Internet

According to the Bureau of Labor Statistics, for 2004, 67 percent of computer programmers held a college or higher degree in 2004, and about 1 in 5 held a graduate degree. Internet Service Providers as an occupation includes 81,000 people, with 29 percent being women. Computer programmers total 564,000 people, 26 percent of whom are women; software engineers include 813,000 people with 25 percent women; computer support specialists total 325,000 with 29 percent women; computer scientists and systems analysts total 700,000 with 29 percent women; network and computer systems administrators include 190,000 with 20 percent women; and network systems and data communications analysts include 312,000 people with 21 percent women.

What do people do for careers connected with the internet? Programmers are employed mostly in software publishing, computer systems design and related services, insurance carriers, data processing, hosting and related services and management of companies. Salaries average for college graduates $50,820 a year in 2005. (It is no wonder that there is only a 30 percent average in the occupations previously listed regarding internet and computer technology). The problem is that women do not gravitate to the computer science major. According to the U.S. Department of Education, 56 percent of college students were women in the year 2000; those reporting computer science as majors were 6 percent women and 13 percent men, similar to the engineering major with 2 percent women and 11 percent men.[16] Currently, the situation for college graduates in computer science is in jeopardy but interest is slowly increasing in computer programming for women students.

There is a projection by the US Commerce Department that there will be a 1.6 million-job vacancy between 2002 and 2012 in Information Technology. It is not surprising then when we hear about hiring practices of internationals, more especially from India where there seems to be an abundance of computer tech people. At fall semester 2005, there were reported 7,952 new Computer Science majors in the U.S.[17]

The following defines what the various fields of occupation encompass.

- **Computer science/programming**—This is a huge field across the university; computer science graduates usually leave with a degree in one hand and a good-paying job in the other. The problem that programmers have, however, is that the curriculum studied usually does not focus on writing, so many companies can't acquire both a programmer and a writer all in one. Hence, people who can write learn how to write for the web but not program—that is invent programs for companies. And here we have another problem. People who graduate with good writing backgrounds—English or History for example—are not necessarily the graphic design types. Graphic design majors learn how to design web pages but not write major content nor invent major programs. What we have then for careers regarding the internet are three types of degreed people: **the computer science (programmer) types, the writers and the art or graphic design types**. Where exactly do they then land jobs. They work for companies that are in the business of programs that computers must follow to perform certain functions. They conceive, design and test logical structures for solving problems by computers. They are creative in the way in which they can "tell" the computers how to compute (financial data) and spell and write (spell and grammatical checks). A computer then is merely a piece of machinery that sits idly by until a programmer gives it orders.
- **Writers**—They graduate from college with experience in writing and editing and can acquire jobs in publishing (newspapers, magazines, books or web publishing in advertising and public relations companies).
- **Graphic designers**—They work for companies whose main purpose is to design ads, brochures, book covers, booklets, annual report covers, or magazine art work of all types. [This next category is our own]
- **Web Technicians**—They work for companies on their web pages, updating, inputting new data, changing links; they are trained specifically for a company's web technology. They could be working in animation or uploading video features to existing web pages. They do not have to be educated in com-

puter programming. Usually they are college educated but can come from practically any degree background.

# Women's Careers in the Computer Industry and the Internet

Dale Spender, who uses the term "nattering on the net" in the title of her text by the same name, states that according to a report in *Digital Media* in 1995, only seven percent of American universities' computer science and engineering faculty were women.[18] So few women are also going into academia to teach computer science and engineering.

Remember, the 2004 report of employed persons published by the Bureau of Labor Statistics shows that in computer-related occupations (scientists, systems analysts, programmers and software engineers), less than 30 percent of these jobs are filled by women. So we should expect to find internet companies with few women as executives and on the boards as well.

Dale Spender considers the reasons:

One, the aversion to the hardware is that women, traditionally, have been taught there is nothing feminine in a machine. Women, traditionally, did not rush to repair typewriters nor were they encouraged to do so, and this conditioning, this socialization role they have been taught is still maintained today. Modern technology, Spender concludes, had also become gendered.[19] Two, designers of hardware and software are not usually female.[20] [And we, the authors of this text, would add that computer hardware design is pretty color-blinded into a white, black or grey world. Apple tried its blue, magenta and green Macs a few years back, but they did not last long. Now, Mac is trying to entice women again with colorful iSkins, which are pink and blue covers for the keyboard; then there's Speck, which is see-through covers for the iMac and come in pink, aqua and red. Hooray for Apple!]

In a longitudinal study by Margolis and Fisher (2002) of 100 computer science students at Carnegie Mellon from 1995 through each student's graduation, they found that women who opt for a major in the computing field come with different forms of attachment, such as wanting the degree so they can work in specific fields, such as environmental pollution or space exploration or biogenetics unlike male students who are in the computer programming major for computer programming, period. This finding then affected the way the degree program was later taught at Carnegie-Mellon; they implemented a more interdisciplinary approach to their courses and enrollment subsequently increased.[21]

While women may not be gravitating toward the degree in computer science/engineering, they are heavy users. There are some very positive internet connections for women today, such as literally thousands of women's groups on-line with informational resources for women globally. In one such women's network, "Virtual Sisterhood," women are connected from Senegal, Malaysia, Sri Lanka, Bangladesh, India, Brazil, Peru, Mexico, Argentina, Costa Rica, Uruguay, Chile, Tunisia, West Bank and Gaza, Canada, the former Soviet block and of course, the USA.

Raphael (2002) also reports that women take greater advantage of email to maintain relationships with friends than men and are more likely to use computer applications for word processing, graphic design and communication. And interestingly enough, he writes that there are more multimedia games designed by women-led companies for girls, although girls still buy only 12 percent of games.[22]

With broadband, fiber optics, high definition, TiVo and video on demand, the future for women in "new media" offers several new opportunities. Colleges are offering a new major called New Media which is attracting as many women as men. In this major, students study communication technologies created by the convergence of computers and traditional media technologies (print, still photography, audio and video).[23] Perhaps this media convergence will even the playing field with respect to women, computers and the internet.

One very successful cyberspace women's network is "Women in Touch": Communication and Help WITCH, where, in a two-week period, narratives from women could be posted about getting connected to cyberspace. Spender states that when she reviewed many of the narratives, one finding was the number of women who mentioned the pleasure of "nattering on the net."[24]

We've chosen to spotlight a woman for whom computer programming and web technology are not frightening at all but who ended up with a career in the technical field by accident.

# Spotlight

Jean French is a lecturer for the Department of Computer Science at Coastal Carolina University; she is working on her Ph.D. in computer programming.

*I never planned a career in computers and didn't major in the field until I started the Ph.D. program. I was always surrounded by computers and considered them a hobby. I finally developed a deep interest in WEB programming while working on my master's degree. I began to educate myself in the field by asking friends questions about programming and buying every book I could. I practiced programming every chance I had. When I was hired for my first WEB programming position, I was still in the learning process. Because programming languages are always changing, I'm still learning today I have been a programmer since 2001 and am thrilled to have transitioned to academics. I am sharing my enthusiasm with students and am trying to show them that the field of computer science is both approachable and exciting, My proudest moment in academics was the day that I heard a biology student had changed majors to computer science after taking my introductory course. The great thing about my field is that I can use skills in and out of the classroom. When I'm not teaching, I volunteer my programming skills for friends, family and charity. It's a dynamic and rewarding career.*

## How to Get Started in Internet Careers

Most certainly higher education will be involved. Computer programming continues to be in demand; anyone graduating from college today in both programming, web design or new media is just about guaranteed to get a job and probably one paying well before they even finish their degree. Women are entering into the field but as we indicated above, slowly. Still, institutional technical departments called IT are found within every major corporation, and there are more and more female IT service reps. We are told that in order to keep up with industry trends, software and hardware changes, continuing educational classes are a must for the career. We've named many companies in this chapter, so finding a job should not be too difficult; being qualified will take work.

# Hollywood and the Internet

Hollywood has always been suspicious of technology and the world wide web gave them new cause for concern. At the onset they scrambled to find enough knowledgeable and trained workers to make them players in the world of the internet. It was during that same time that we heard about the "skateboard CEO's." They were the young college graduates who felt very comfortable with computers and new software. But, the large movie studios had other concerns.

They watched while armies of executives jumped ship and either left completely to get a piece of that big internet pie, or just find board positions on e-businesses. They left studios, agencies and networks and they transferred their creativity from on-screen entertainment to online entertainment.

Another big studio concern was over what would happen to distribution as they knew it when anyone would have an opportunity to download a movie? What about copyright protection? According to the firm, Reciprocal, of the $170 billion worth of digitizable content available in 1999, only about 13% of it was available online; by 2004 25% of it, including movies and TV shows, would be one click away.[25]

In August of 2001, the Moviefly venture formed by MGM, Sony, Paramount, Universal and Warner Bros. was their answer. They shared the multi-million dollar cost to avoid prior failed attempts by individual studios and built the infrastructure. "The studios recognize the handwriting on the wall. Online video is coming," said Probe Research analyst Walter Miao. "Rather than react negatively to it, they've decided to try to develop it on their own and see how much of a market they can make."[26]

The boom of the internet in the late 1990s, led to a crash by 2001. A publication called the Industry Standard reported that from January 2000 to April 2001, 90,000 workers were laid off from "Internet economy" firms. More recent figures are not available from that publication; like the dot-coms it covered, the Industry Standard went bust.[27] In that same article from 2003, the research firm Webmergers.com estimates that there once were 7,000-10,000 funded Internet companies of all stripes. In 2000, 225 shut down, last year 544 more closed. So far this year, 126 online companies have shuttered, and 3,700 mergers and acquisitions also have thinned the herd since 2000.[28]

Several of those Hollywood executives who jumped ship at the onset of the internet rush, wanted to get their old jobs back after their new companies failed, but were afraid that the studios would not take them back. But, as the studios moved to make their individual websites profitable, it was to their advantage to rehire those who were already successful in the movie business and now had all that new knowledge to share. For many it became a win-win.

As for the movie studios concerns about and distribution and piracy, they continue to struggle with ways to make it work for all concerned. Beth Minchart, executive vp international new media at NBC Universal International Television distribution is looking toward new deals that would introduce network series to the international market within days after they are broadcast in the U.S. She is among several network executives trying to combat foreign piracy.[29]

And, in January 2007, Netflix began an Internet movies-on-demand service that makes it a more direct competitor with the likes of Movielink and CinemaNow, two early services that rent films for viewing on computer screens. They call it WatchNow.[30]

# Minority Women in the Internet Industry

Where are they? In corporate operations for AOL, Tiane Mitchell Gordon, is Vice President of Diversity and Inclusion. Her job is to promote diversity in the company. In a 2004 interview captured from HR Innovator[31] magazine, Ms. Mitchell Gordon stated that AOL's principles center around collaboration, execution, leadership, innovation and accountability; further that she would add "inclusion" to those principles. And Mitchell Gordon quotes a scene from the movie, The Color Purple, when Celia says to Mister, "Until you do right by me, all that you ever do will fail."

With respect to corporate ownership of mass media, we believe that until minority voices have much more presence in all venues of mass media, including media and entertainment companies, such as AOL, as humanists they will ever fail.

However, even white women are scarce in computer related industry. Jane Margolis (previously cited) was asked this question: "Is there any evidence of a bias against women computer programmers?" To which she replied, "Well, I think that the expectations from parents, teachers and students themselves is that a computer scientist looks a certain way." When she asked students to describe their fellow computer science students, they said that these students all work at the computer 24/7. "They live and breathe it. They only emerge with a monitor tan. They just love it in their bones." But when she asked male CS majors about this, they responded that the image did not fit them at all.

According to the BLS 2005 employment census, only 34,000 Black or African American women work in computer systems design and related services out of a total employment population of 1,632,000. On a graduate degree level, students acquiring advanced degrees in CS are even less than 20%, so the question to ask is how much effect will fewer women professors in CS have on female student enrollment, especially minority women?

## The Internet and the Glass Ceiling

It is difficult to claim a glass ceiling exists for women in the internet-industry when such low percentages of women are opting for college careers in computer science or engineering fields. Perhaps colleges are not actively recruiting women for the major; perhaps the major is filled to the brim with international students who pay large sums of money for US education. We can only withhold an opinion for now. Yet, there are not many women in the companies shown in Table 10.1. Should we claim that because women just are not attracted to computer programming, i.e., software development and web page design they are naturally not hired in these companies? That would not hold up if we look at a genre like Magazines, where even in those companies with holdings in mostly women's magazines, we don't see women in the very top management. The same could be said about all of mass media venues. Of course, then we point to a very interesting woman who certainly understands the power of the internet, Meg Whitman.

## Diversified Diva: Meg Whitman

We are naming our diva here based on the power of the company she heads that attracts millions of consumers. Diva Meg Whitman is current CEO of *e*Bay.com. The following excerpts help introduce Ms. Whitman.

BusinessWeek online, May 15, 2000: Meg Whitman, CEO of pioneering auctioneer eBay, Inc., remains the czarina of Net auctions—and that's saying a lot. Three tough competitors, Amazon.com, Yahoo! and Lycos tried to knock eBay from its perch. It didn't happen.

Salon.com November 27, 2001: When Meg Whitman took over as chief executive of eBay some three years ago, she set about her work with her usual mixture of know-how and curiosity. She knew she had to build the eBay brand. But she also listened to the auction site's founders and conferred closely with them. Her style—collaborative yet decisive, serious but loose—set the tone.

U.S. News & World Report, October 31, 2005: Meg Whitman leads by not leading, bosses by not bossing, and manages by not managing. Yet the 49-year-old CEO of eBay presides over company that has been described as growing faster in its first decade than any other enterprise in the history of capitalism. Since Whitman joined eBay in early 1998, its revenue has exploded—from about $5.7 million to an expected $4.3 *billion* this year, 2006. The first global online marketplace to connect buyers and sellers 24-7, eBay conducts more transactions every day than the Nasdaq Stock Market.

Besides the fact that she is in charge of 9,300 employees and 157 million customers, the answer is that she has diversified herself by being involved in the youngest of the mass media, the internet. Also, she is on the board of DreamWorks Animation, discussed in the movie chapter, and formerly served as an executive for Walt Disney Co. Also, Whitman is a master of the art of branding. She has done for eBay what the other divas mentioned in this text have done with their names. She used advertising to launch the idea of online auctions and competes heavily with Amazon.com in the sale of books, movies and music (CDs). She takes advantage of opportunities to brag about eBay's successes; for example, she was quick to advertise in mass media outlets the fact that eBay had sold for Warner Brothers the boat used in the film, *The Perfect Storm,* at a price of $145,000.[32]

She sometimes answers customers emails herself and she is a billionaire; she has raised two children and is married to a neurosurgeon. She seems to have the gift for juggling priorities and remaining loyal to the company she is constantly reinventing. This alone makes her quite a diversified diva.

# Summary

If women continue to shy away from computers and cyberspace technology, changes on web sites, designed by male engineers mostly, will be slight. Unlike the rest of mass media, where women have tried to get footholds in executive career tracks, the aversion to computer technology may be accidental. When computer programming becomes more creative, at least in women's eyes, gender changes in labor will take place.

For now, as we have discussed, those that control cyberspace, the internet, software and hardware of computers are again mostly white males. A Meg Whitman is rare indeed and right now a popular role model for women.

Yet, women are the heavies in terms of usage. Women are also connected internationally. Eventually, the weight of this consumerism will produce even greater results. For now, we have whole networks for women; they can create change for each other by merely talking to each other, even if they never meet in person.

*Table 9.1. List of Internet-related Companies*

| Company | Price per share of stock | CEO | Notable Products | Number of Executives | Number of Board Members | Highest Clout Position of a Woman |
|---|---|---|---|---|---|---|
| AOL Time Warner renamed Time Warner in 2003[33] | $14.59 TWX | Randy Falco, AOL | Aol.com, Netscape, CompuServe MapQuest Moviefone | 9 (2 are women) on executive team, AOL | Time Warner Board of Directors: 11 (2 are women) | Tiane Mitchell Gordon, Sr. Vice Pres., Diversity & Inclusion, AOL |
| Apple | $126.61 AAPL | Steve Jobs | iMac, iPod, MacBook | 10 men (0 women) | 8 men (0 women) | NA |
| Google | $437.92 GOOG | Dr. Eric Schmidt | Google.com | 10 (1 woman) | 14 (1 woman) | Shona Brown, Sr. VP, Business Operations |
| Microsoft | $27.96 MSFT | Steven Ballmer | Microsoft Office, Explorer, MSN | 16 (2 are women) | 10 (2 are women) | Dina Dublon, Member of the Board; |
| Yahoo! | $26.71 YHOO | Terry Semel | Yahoo.com | 6 (1 woman) | 10 men (0 women) | Susan Decker, Chief Financial Officer and Executive VP, Finance and Administration |

Compiled with information from corporate web pages March 14, 2008

# Notes

1.  "Internet Usage Worldwide by Country, 2007." www.infoplease.com/ipa/A0933606.html.

2.  Report: Demographics. Pew/Internet. www.pewinternet.org/PPF/r/171/report_display.asp.

3.  The Internet Society explains this at www.isoc.org/internet/history/brief.shtml.

4.  See www.learnframe.com/aboutelearning/page17.asp.

5.  See www.cyberjournalist.net/news/003674.php.

6.  "Media Report to Women." *Industry Statistics.* December 2005. (www.mediareporttowomen.com).

7.  Go to www.vault.com/nr/printable.jsp?ch_id=253&article_id=2625047&print=1.

8.  Marketing to Women: Addressing Women and Women's Sensibilities (2005). September,V18, i9p1(2).

9.  Known for his idea that television would create a global village, McLuhan died at the beginning of the computer age and the internet concept was not born.

10. From Netsmartz.org.

11. Baig, Edward C. (2004). "Tired of Internet Explorer's risks? Try one of these browsers." *USA Today*, July 7; posted online at www.usatody.com/tech/colummnist/edwardbaig/2004-07-07-baig_x.htm.

12. Go to it at www.microsoft.com/msft/reports/ar05/staticversion/10k_sl_eng.html.

13. Go to www.finance.yahoo.com/q?s=aapl&d=t.

14. Go to http://yahoo.client.shareholder.com/press/overview.cfm.

15. Ibid.

16. NCES.ed.gov/pubs2002/2002.68pdf.

17. Vegso, Jay (2006). "Drop in CS Bachelor's Degree Production." Computing Research Association, published originally in March 2006 Vol. 18, No. 2; online at www.cra.org/CRN/articles/march06/vegso.html.

18. Dale Spender. *Nattering on the Net: Women, Power and Cyberspace.* (North Melbourne, Australia: Spinifex Press, 1995), p. 200.

19. Spender, p. 175.

20. Spender, p. 171.

21. Gilbert, Alorie (2002). Newsmaker: Computer science's gender gap. CNET News com, February 8, 2002 located at www.news.com/2008-1082-833090.html.

22. Raphael, Chad (2002). Citizen Jane: Rethinking design principles for closing the gender gap in computing. ED-MEDIA 2002 World conference on Educational Multimedia, Hypermedia & Telecommunications. Proceedings (14th) Denver, Colorado, June 24-29.

23. This information found on California State University, Dr. Paul Martin Lester's page about New Media Curriculum: http://commfaculty.fullerton.edu/lester/curriculum/newmedia.htm.

24. Spender, p. 238.

25. THR Reciprocal survey, August 1-7, 2000.

26. Internetweek.com, August 23, 2001. "Is Hollywood Net-ready" by Jade Boyd.

27. THR Internet Survivors, December 31, 2002-January 6, 2003 by Paul Bond.

28. Ibid.

29. THR October 5-7, 2007 VOD to the rescue for TV.

30. THR January 16-22, 2007, p. 2.

31. See this interview on www.marthafinney.com/HRInnovator/2004-06.html.

32. See Salon.com at http://archive.salon.com/people/bc/2001/11/27/whitman/index1.html.

33. Press release is dated September 18,2003 and can be seen at http://press.aol.com/article_display.cfm?article_id=401.

# Chapter Ten

# Media Divas and Beyond

**D**iva was a term used to describe a distinguished female opera singer. But, more recently it came to include popular female performers of non-operatic works. It derives from an Italian word meaning "goddess," which, in turn derives from the feminine form of a Latin word *divus*, meaning "divine one." The Oxford English dictionary reads—noun, a celebrated female opera singer. Origin Latin, "goddess."

*Time Magazine* observed in its October 21, 2002 issue: "By definition, a *diva* is a rampaging female ego redeemed only in part by a lovely voice." The word was originally used for great female opera singers, almost always sopranos, but can be used to describe many female celebrities, such as singers, or movie actresses.

As with earlier "prima donnas," which was also derived from opera (lit. "first lady"), the term has slipped from its trade origins and come to be used in any theatrical or performance setting. In particular, because of marketing efforts, the word "diva" has come to be applied most often to popular female performers. In order to qualify as a diva there must be one, or both, of two dominant traits present: a broad and expansive voice and/or a thoroughly captivating and commanding stage presence."[1]

Some women have even been given titles. Like Tina Turner who is The Queen of Rock and Aretha Franklin, dubbed the Queen of Soul. Donna Summer is the Queen of Disco, Mary J. Blige is the Queen of Hip-Hop, Gloria Estefan is the Queen of Latin Pop, Madonna is the Queen of Pop, while Britney Spears and Christina Aquilera are the Princesses of Pop.[2]

In any case, the term *Diva* is used to describe a woman of rare outstanding talent. When we look at women in media careers we feel many women over the years have not only showed outstanding talent but have made a name for themselves in their fields. Some have even become household names.

# Media Divas

Our definition of **Media Diva** would be a woman who has enjoyed success in her chosen field, including women like we've listed here:

**Barbara Walters** started as a newswriter for CBS. But before long she moved to the Today Show and eventually became known as the Today Show girl. She moved to ABC and became the first woman co-anchor on a nightly newscast with Harry Reasoner and was known for years on the ABC newsmagazine 20/20. She expanded her field of expertise in interviewing as the co-creator and co-executive producer of *The View,* a controversial talk show where she serves as one of the hosts.

**Diane Sawyer**, co-host of Good Morning America, has been a leading newswoman for many years. In 2001 *Ladies Home Journal* named her as one of the 30 most powerful women in America. Her news reporting days began on the local TV network, WLKY-TV in Louisville, Kentucky. She moved to CBS as a political correspondent and became the co-anchor of the *CBS Morning News.* Now at ABC, she first served as co-anchor on *Primetime Live* and by 1999 had begun her current role as the co-anchor of *Good Morning America.*

**Sherry Lansing**, a behind-the-camera *Diva* in movies, is the former CEO of Paramount and was the first woman to head a major studio. Although she started out acting, she decided early in her career that her future was behind the camera. She was the first female President of 20th Century Fox and moved to Paramount where she enjoyed success for twelve years with such hits as *Titanic, Braveheart* and *Forest Gump.* She is currently a Regent of the University of California.

**Nora Roberts** is a *Media Diva* in book publishing. Her books have been published in at least 25 different countries. Prolific is hardly the word for Roberts, who also, by the way, publishes under J.D. Robb. She has many books in print right now: *O'Hurley's Return, Black Rose, Northern Lights, Calhouns, MacKade Brothers, Reunion, Moon Shadows, Heaven and Earth, Heart of the Sea, Blue Dahlia, Macgregor Grooms, Winner Takes All* and *Gabriel's Angel* and then there are her novels written with her psuedonym, J. D. Robb.

**Toni Morrison** is a *Media Diva* also worth mentioning. In the 1960 she was at one time a senior editor at Random House and started writing during that time. She has written *The Bluest Eye* (1970), *Sua* (1973), *Song of Solomon* (1977), *Tar Baby* (1981) and *Beloved* (1988). She won all types of awards, the National Book Award, the National Book Critic's Award, the American Academy and Institute of Arts and Letters Award and the Pulitzer Prize for fiction in 1988. She published *Jazz* in 1992 and Paradise in 1998. She received the Nobel Peace Prize in Literature in 1993. Today, she teaches at Princeton University.

We can't leave the publishing world without mention of **J. K. Rowling** again. She is a person who with determination and little finances established a well-known character, Mr. Harry Potter, and a whole realm of wonderful wizardly people, enough to put her into the category of millionaire (she received $4,000 for her first Potter book in 1997, $30 million for her 2000 Potter book; and between those three years received $400 million). Rowling is to be admired for her fortitude in writing and her creative genius for her characters. She is a *Diva* who stands apart from the crowd.

A *Diva* in the world of magazines worth noting is **Helen Gurley Brown** (1922- 2001) who was editor-in-chief of Cosmopolitan for 32 years. She turned Cosmo into a highly successful magazine for women in the 1960s when she boldly wrote and talked about sex. She had already published Sex and the Single Girl in 1962. She became well known for her advocacy of sexual freedom for women and wanted Cosmo to be their guide. She was a diva beyond divas in the magazine world.

A newspaper *Diva* worth noting is **Katharine Graham** (1917-2001) who became the publisher of *The Washington Post* after her husband, Philip Graham died in 1963. The Post had been her father's company prior to her marriage to Graham, so it was fitting that she took control after her husband's death. She had also previously been a newswoman. She knew the in's and out's of publishing the paper, She became nationally known during the Watergate scandal when her reporters, Carl Bernstein and Robert Woodward broke the story of Nixon's involvement. She was courageous and brought considerable economic power to the Post during her years as publisher.

**Sheryl Sandberg** was vice president of global online sales and operations at Google, in 2006. She's a Harvard graduate and was included in Fortune's 50 Most Powerful Women of 2007 at the age of 38 was the youngest on the list. In March of 2008 she left Google to become Facebook's Chief Operations Officer.

**Christine Fix** is the Editor-In -Chief of Reality TV Magazine and is or was editor of Soaps.com. The January 2008 page for Reality TV Magazine states that it is a leading online publication covering everything you need to know about your favorite reality TV show since June 2003. There are several articles on Soaps.com with Fix's name attached including a blog. Clearly she is diva-moving in the online genre of media.

**Anne Perlman** is President and CEO of Moai Technologies. She says "I've never hit my head on a glass ceiling that I've known . . . I've always assumed gender neutrality."[3] In another article about her she said that she did experience a women's restroom shortage while in business school at the University of California at Los Angeles where only 22 percent of her 1976 MA class was female. She joined Moai in 1997 after having been an independent consultant. Moai is all about strategic sourcing, including hosted sourcing software.[4]

Obviously there are many more women in each of these areas who have gained high levels of success in their own medium and we believe deserve the title of *Media Diva.* But, we don't stop here.

There are those women wearing two hats, who have been successful actresses and went on to form their own production companies, like **Meg Ryan** who formed Prufrock with Nina Sadowsky**; Jodie Foster** who owns Egg Pictures with Meg LaFauve; **Drew Barrymore** who owns Flower Films with Nancy Juvonen; **Marilyn Monroe,** certainly a noted icon, who formed Marilyn Monroe Productions with fashion photographer Milton Greene; **Julia Roberts** who's Red Om which is her husband Danny's last name spelled backwards and **Reese Witherspoon,** who won the Oscar for her leading role in *Walk the Line,* and has finally reached the highest salary for a female on the big screen (equal to Julia Roberts' highest) also owns her own production company called Type A.

And then there are other *dual-titled Media Divas*, not just actor/producers, but those who we consider to be hyphenates like those who can call themselves writer/director, actor/director, and of course, producer/director. They do all this, while remaining in the same medium, usually film. Women like **Nora Ephron** who wrote screenplays, then became a successful director is another example.

All of these women found success wearing different hats in the same medium.

## Multi-Media Divas

But let's go beyond these *dual-titled Media Divas* who multi-task in their own mediums to those who crossover to other mediums. Like **Cokie Roberts** who first became well known in radio, then moved to television and enjoyed continued success, even before she became an author; or Cathleen Black who can easily jump from magazines to newspapers. She is currently president of Hearst Magazines (publishes *Cosmopolitan, Esquire, Good, Housekeeping* and *Harper's Bazaar)*. She ventured over to USA Today for a few years and then landed the power position at Hearst; or **Katie Couric**, who is the newest and only regular Nightly News female anchor as well as managing editor on a major network, *The CBS Evening News*. Starting out as desk assistant at ABC News in Washington, DC, she continued behind the camera at CNN and then became a general assignment reporter for WRC-TV. She spent fifteen years as co-host on *The Today Show,* before accepting her current anchoring duties. But not before she crossed over to another medium as an author of childrens books. **Carol Burnett** opened in her off-Broadway musical *Once Upon A Mattress* in 1959 and then enjoyed a long career in television comedy, wrote a book about her career, and just last year co-produced and starred in a new version of the musical for DVD release.

We like to think of these *Media Divas* that have become successful in more than one medium as *Multi-Media Divas*. Other examples of those in this category would be women like **Lucille Ball** who began on Broadway and moved quickly into films, getting the title of Queen of B's because of so many B movies she starred in, like *Five Came Back*. Her weekly radio program, *My Favorite Husband,* garnered such a successful rating that it became the famous television sitcom, *I Love Lucy*. She won four of her 13 Emmy nominations, and she was the first woman in television to be head of a production studio—Desilu. She is also recognized in another medium as an author, her latest biography & autobiography is none other than *I Love Lucy,* a 1997 release of a work penned thirty years earlier.

Another example of a *Multi-Media Diva* would be **Rosie O'Donnell** who began as a popular comedian on stage, then acted in films like *League of Their Own* and became a successful television talk show host, then created her own magazine and finally became a Broadway show producer. Her first novel was a memoir, *Find Me* and her latest is *Celebrity Detox*.

While **Mary Tyler Moore** is primarily know for her roles in sitcoms and television shows. From the Dick Van Dyke Show to the Mary Tyler Moor Show she earned seven Emmy Awards. She did cross over to film and her most notable film role for which she was nominated for an Oscar as best actress was in Ordinary People. As co-founder of MTM Enterprises with her former husband, Grant Tinker, she produced such spin-offs from the Mary Tyler Moore Show as Rhoda and Phyllis.

Another *Multi-Media Diva* is **Eleanor Clift.** She began as a journalist for Newsweek first in Atlanta then in Washingotn DC She had a short stint at the Los Angeles Times but returned to Newsweek as deputy bureau chief in Washington. She is a regular panelist on The McLaughlin Group, a syndicated TV show and a political analyst for Fox News Network. She and her husband have written two books together: *War Without Bloodshed: The Art of Politics* (1996) and *Madam President: Shattering the Last Glass Ceiling* (2000). She also contributes to *More*, a magazine for women over 50.

**Maureen Dowd** won the Pulitzer Prize for commentary in 1999 for her columns about Clinton and the Monica Lewinsky affair. She first wrote for time magazine then the now defunct Washington Star; then she joined the New York Times in 1983. She is known for her acid wit and withering attacks on Clinton. In 2994 she released her first book called *Bushworld: Enter at Your Own Risk.* Then another followed in 2005, *Are Men Necessary? When Sexes Collide.*

**Ellen Goodman** is nationally known as a columnist, a Pulitzer Prize winning one while at the *Boston Globe* in 1980. The award was for Distinguished Commentary. She is syndicated and we can usually read her columns in most major newspapers. According to the National Society of Newspaper Columnists, her columns are published in 375 newspapers across the county. She has also written several books of non-fiction; some are book editions of her columns. One recent book is called *I know what you mean* and is about the power of friendship in women's lives. (Simon & Schuster, 2000).

Another interesting diva that we claim fits into the category of *Multi-Media Diva* is **Monica Lozano.** If you haven't heard of her, you will eventually. This is a diva on the move. She is president and chief operating officer of La Opinión, the largest daily Spanish-language newspaper in the country. She is also in charge of the magazine they now publish under the La Opinión direction as well as digital online news. She is vice president of Communications, Inc., the newspaper's parent company.

She is also on the executive team of ImpreMedia, which is an advertising company that serves 2.2 million online visitors per month and gets ads into newspapers in Hispanic markets. In her 50s, she is so well known that she has leaped into various organizations, serving on a multitude of board of directors including Walt Disney Co., heath and cultural organizations, banks, universities. She is also a member of the Board of Regents of the University of California. She is a diversified diva to watch.

Another with talents as a *Multi-Media Diva* is **Tina Brown**. Here, we have an interesting woman who has moved from magazine editor of the British *Tatler* to editor-in-chief of *Vanity Fair* to editor of *The New Yorker*, to founder of *Talk Magazine* with Harvey Weinstein (as in the brothers, Bob and Harvey Weinstein). On a side note, Weinstein and Brown apparently did not get along. Weinstein bought her contract for $1 Million in 2002.[5] Not to worry, this diva moves fast. She went on to host CNBC, *A Talk Show with Tina Brown.* from 2003-2005 to writing a definitive book, *The Diana Chronicles* about Princess Diana, releasd in 2007. What's next?

Finally, we suggest that there is yet another level to which these women rise . . . to the level of a *Diversified Diva*, some of whom we already introduced you to at the end of each of the preceeding chapters. It could be said that these women brand themselves.

We introduced you to some of them already, like Martha Stewart who branded her name with her products at Macy's; and the Olsen twins with their clothing line. We'd liker to suggest a few more women who we feel have became a brand, like **Sarah Jessica Parker**, who started in Broadway as Little Orphan Annie. She moved to television in 1982 as one of the leads in *Square Pegs*. After her role in Steve Martin's film *L A Story,* she was cast as lead actress in the popular *Sex and the City* series that catapulted her into such films as *State and Main,* and the more recent *Failure to Launch*. The long awaited film *Sex and the City is* slated to open in spring 08. Her newest endeavor (here comes the branding theory) is her clothing line *Bitten,* which promises to be affordable to the average woman.

The August 22, 2005 issue of Time Magazine releases their telephone poll which documents the fact that the U. S. Hispanic population increased to 41.3 million and Hispanics are projected to account for 46% of all U.S. population growth over the next 20 years.[6] Our research did not find that Hispanic women in media came close to those numbers. But it is interesting that when we look at *Media Divas,* we find two who fall in the *Diversified Media category,* including Time Magazine's choice of one of the 25 most influential Hispanics[7]—The Diva from the Block— **Jennifer Lopez**.

The girl from the Bronx, broke all charts with her albums and found success on the radio with her music; then became know for films like *Maid in Manhattan*, O*ut of Sight, Gigli* and *The Wedding Planner*, then became a producer with her husband Marc Anthony of their own company; and finally created her own products, JLO by Jennifer Lopez, her clothing line and a fragrance line including *Glow*. All this has made her the 19th richest person under 40, according to Fortune Magazine.

Another of our choices for **Diversified Diva**, also a Hispanic female listed in that same Time Magazine issue of the 25 most influential Hispanics is **Christina Saralegui**, the host of a weekly prime-time show, El Show de Christina, from her studio in Miami. She has provided 16 years of programming on the Univision Network. Compared often to Oprah, she sits at the center of a Hispanic empire. In 1991 she premiered her magazine *Christina LaRevista*. Her talk show has received double digit Emmys. She has a new clothing line and has received accolades for her "Casa Christina," furniture line (both of which we consider to be part of her branding). Her bilingual website receives a half million hits a day and like Oprah, has established a foundation. "Up With Life" provides HIV education for kids. She is proud of the fact that her mother was always liberated and her father knew how to knit and did all the cooking.[8]

How could we complete a book about women in the media without highlighting the most **Diversified Diva** of all time.

**Oprah Winfrey**, the founder and Chairman of Harpo Entertainment Group and the founder of the soon to air cable television outlet OWN (Oprah Winfrey Network) started as a part-time radio announcer at WVOL before she was hired as a reporter/anchor for WTVF-TV in Nashville. She moved to WJZ in Baltimore and added talk shows to her busy schedule as the Host of *People are Talking,* while continuing to anchor the news. It wasn't long before she moved to Chicago to host AM Chicago, and after turning the little watched show into first place in the ratings, she premiered *The Oprah Winfrey Show* which became nationally syndicated in 1986. In February 2006 she launched "Oprah & Friends", a satellite radio channel on XM. Her latest primetime network offering is Oprah's Big Give on ABC. Her work in film includes acting in *The Color Purple,* producing and acting in *Beloved*. Harpo (Oprah spelled backwards) Productions has released several film and television projects, and most recently she was a producer for *The Great Debaters* starring Denzel Washington. She publishes two magazines, *O, The Oprah Magazine* and *O at Home*. Her Angel Network funded Seven Fountains Primary School in KwaZulu-Natal, South Africa. While becoming newsworthy for some staffing problems initially, it promises to educate a new generation of women leaders. Time Magazine's April 30, 2006 edition says "she has purpose-an abiding commitment to the principles of goodness and generosity that transcend any individual." Authors around the world vie to get her approval for their books.

## That's It For Now

When we decided to look at women in media careers for each of the categories above, we had no idea how many of them would be worthy of these new titles. As you can see we have only scratched the surface.

How could we name all the divas in the world? Or in the U.S. alone? It is impossible. So many women have become multi-taskers, making money in more than one medium. Columnists for example write books (Diane Woodruff for one); journalists make documentaries (Linda Ellerbee for one); authors end up very rich because their books are adapted for the screen (J.K. Rowling or previously Agatha Christie); some writers end up playwrights (Toni Morrison for one). So it goes on and on.

Our only hope is that it will be possible to add more women to the *Diversified Diva* category in our next edition.

(Meanwhile, check this web page out for a list of notable women in media: www.infoplease.com/spot/whmbios11.html).

## Notes

1. *Time Magazine*, October 21, 2002.
2. Ibid.
3. This is from Informationweek.com, April 28, 2008.
4. See two articles about Anne Perlman and Moai Technologies: www.moal.com/corporate/corporate_overview.asp and www.informationweek.com/807/perlman.htm.
5. Carr, David and David D. Kirkpatrick (2002). "The Media Business; Miramax Buys Out Tina Brown For an Estimated $1 Million." *The New York Times*, July 24. (See this at http://query.nytimes.com/gst/fullpage.html?res= 9902E3DA1238F937A15754COA9649C8863).

6. Time Magazine telephone poll conducted July 29–August 3, 2005 of 503 Latino adults. See the results at www.srbi.com/time_poll_arc17.html.

7. "The 25 Most Influential Hispanics in America." *Time Magazine*, Aug. 13, 2005. www.time.com/time/nation/printout/o,8816,1093637,00.html.

8. Ibid. See her book, *Christina, My Life as a Blonde*, Time Warner on Demand, 1998.

# Chapter Eleven

# What's Up With the Techno Future?

What we have tried to state in this text is the fact that while it is apparent that at the very top tier of the conglomerates there is firmly in place a glass ceiling, women are nevertheless continuing to climb that media ladder. We have pointed out how women are in top management positions in all mass media venues, with the possible exception of internet providers such as Google and Yahoo (Chapter 9, Table 9.1). However, we also pointed out that women are still not very attracted to computers and computer programming in general. In fact, technical support jobs for women are plentiful, but not many women apply.

The internet is a source for all of mass media. Major newspapers are online. One editor of a daily told us they were in dire need of a graphic design/web page layout person who could write. Journalism education is moving toward a future when all news will be online, and the tactile sensation of holding a newspaper will be a thing of the past. That's sad news for us because we are people raised on the morning newspaper. Magazines may hold on for a much longer time because there is something very attractive in seeing a magazine lying around on the coffee table. Yet, electronic reading is here with the birth of Kindle, the new Amazon invention of a 10-ounce hand-held electronic device that can access thousands of newspapers/magazines as well as full book texts. We envision an airport terminal of people standing in line with their Kindles completely absorbed in various text. This will not leave much room for socializing. We find ourselves wondering if indeed the more relational we get with such electronic devices, the laptop, the hand-held electronic book, the IPod, the less we will talk to each other. Now, that's a thought.

Our students in classes are informed computer experts; they can enlighten us about any new gadget and blog site—MySpace, FaceBook, YouTube, Innertube, etc. They can find out about anything within a few seconds on a nearby computer. The internet is their encyclopedia, dictionary, number one reference source and possibly best friend. They certainly rely on the internet for their social life for they are always checking either email or cell phone messages. Going to a library and checking out books is becoming more rare with each generation. The day may well come when all textbooks will be accessible online also. What then will happen to the book?

# Things to Come

As Internet television becomes more of a reality, we wonder what will happen to the television set on the console. Technology is already developed for TV sets to become internet-connected. Brian Rosenberg from iMedia Connection writes this:

> Internet TV is the perfect platform for unrestrained, but carefully watched, content syndication. So long as content is tracked, monetized and quality controlled, trends can be identified that point to how the content is fitting into the lives of its audiences based on where it's being featured or requested from. Ubiquitous video strategy with data on the content-to-content relationship gives every publisher, portal, blog, vlog and social network the ability to provide their audiences with contextuality relevant video and targeted advertising (as sold by a number of parties).[1]

Steve Jobs, CEO of Apple, Inc. is calling Apple TV a DVD player for the 21st Century. The March 2007 launch of Apple TV is basically a set-top device that allows media residing in one's iTunes library—including music, TV shows, feature films and podcasts—to be enjoyed on TV screens. Wirelessly.[2]

The online community is now targeting kids with last year's introduction of Nicktropolis, where kids can customize the appearance of an avatar with which they can navigate a digital world complete with it's own currency.[3]

Jeff Zucker, CEO of NBC Universal is coming to grips with the change in how people will experience TV, but that doesn't mean over-the-air broadcast TV is going to go away. He thinks programming will be available in many different ways and will force change.[4]

Google-owned YouTube announced an agreement in February 2007 with Digital Music Group that made more than 4,000 hours of television and film content available on the video-sharing site. It was the first long form video program YouTube obtained.[5]

One of the newest offerings in media is mobile programming and technology. They are targeting the primary consumer of the miniscreen world; the so-called "early adopters" ages 18-24. Verizon has a new interactive programming guide that allows video customers to access content from the television, Internet and their personal music and photo collections. The following four mobile entertainment providers are vying for a healthy slice of a pie that has yet to be carved.[6]

GoTV: calls itself "the first made-for-mobile television network." It offers 60 hours and more than 300 hours of original programs each month on you phone.

Amp'd Mobile: While this is only available on special Amp'd Mobile pones, it offers repackaged content over originals in its 27 linear channel TV offerings.

MobiTV: This is the largest mobile program subscription service in the world. It offers 50 channels of programming in the U.S. and an additional 100 internationally.

Limbo 41414: This is a text-message-based mobile entertainment gameplay—specifically Limbo Auction. It's an interactive game that is won by bidding the lowest, a very different concept than bidding on ebay.

While print becomes electronic, radio, television and film already digital will become more diverse. There will be more of it to choose from. It is only a matter of time before our flat screen high definition televisions will be able to access film playing in a nearby cinema. Perhaps one day the cinema, the theater, will be also gone.

# The Ever-Changing, Ever-Present Media

These are all mere speculations of course. We are players in the information age and can barely keep up with it. Each time we learn a new software program, figure out how to hookup a new flat-screen, program the iPod, set up an MP3 player, something new is developed and put on the market. Both men and women working in mass media jobs are caught up in a daily milieu of new, new, new!

Jobs are plentiful in media. We have added some examples below. Good writers will find easy access to jobs in all fields. Television news stations always need people who can write for the spoken word and do it fast. All of print media of course depends on good writing. College graduates are in a good place right now if they obtain skills in web technology and happen to be very good writers as well. Better yet, graphic design skills along with the aforementioned will command top salaries. Jeffrey Cole, director of the Center for the Digital Future at the University of Southern California's Annenberg School for Communications, says: " In the very near future, there will be little difference between surfing the Web on your TV and watching TV on your computer. Internet Protocol Television or IPTV, will blur the thin line currently separating both technologies—meaning video programming wherever, whenever, on-demand and in many different formats."7

Naturally, there are problems with the internet. We are already aware of downloading music piracy issues. Another problem is web sites that look authentic (Wikipedia for one) and turn out to be sites that are either mass-edited and therefore made up of multiple writers or websites that look very "medical" and turn out to be a person with supposedly college and certainly no medical degree. This is when the old adage should come in, "Let the User Beware." Caution is given about believing everything that you read on the internet. The very best policy is to understand a site for what it is. Blogs is such a site. It provides all kinds of information, all opinion, but some are noteworthy. Perhaps you have a blog. Here are some blogs we've picked up about the internet and problem issues; you may or may not agree with them:

Bill St. Arnaud writes his blog titled Geo-Blocking: Why Hollywood Is a Major Cause of Piracy. It's about the fact that content downloaded via Apples iTunes and Amazon's UnBox is only available to U.S. citizens because of geo-blocking [blocking content from going beyond our borders]; Mary E. Schaklett writes in Waging War on Internet Piracy that some business owners have invested millions of dollars into websites only to see them pirated and asks, is there any way to stop it?; and Tom Haynes writes in his blog, In the New Networked Economy, Authenticity Is a Category Killer that the world will reach the Jump Point in 2022 with three billion people all connected in a seamless networked economy.

He predicts that in the coming world the most unauthentic brands and companies that are also the most trusted will win. Phonies beware, he writes.[8]

The fact is that it should be of concern that a few conglomerates own the most media outlets. Case in point: Time Warner. Let's look closely at the conglomerate,

Time Warner is the parent company to AOL, Time Warner Cable, HBO, Turner Broadcast, Time, Inc., Warner Brothers and Global Media Group. The women listed in key positions in each subsidiary are found in the table at the end of the chapter (Table 11.1). The chart does not include all other women who work for the TW subsidiaries, others who are probably in some managerial or supervisory roles.

We can see from the table that there are more women in clout positions at Warner Brothers and Time Inc., and only some representation at the other subsidiaries of Time Warner. It will be interesting to keep updating this chart on this one company to see the progression of women in the power positions, for we are confident they will continue to make career pathways. If we were to make such tables for all the conglomerates we have discussed in this text, on an average basis, they would all probably even out. There may not be as many women as we would hope for, but the women are there.

Again, we want to leave you with the idea that women are in key positions in media, which we have tried to make clear throughout this text. We have emphasized college education and in fact most of the women in media jobs that we know do have college backgrounds. Not all women study, for example, journalism or broadcast, and end up working in that very field. One such person is our own manuscript preparation person, Dorothy Albritton. She prepares manuscripts that are "camera ready" for the publisher. She has her own business (Majestic Wordsmith) and loves her job. She told us the following:

*After earning my bachelor's degree in Family Studies in 1985, I got married a week later and immediately took on various office jobs. By 1993 I had been employed for five years at the University Press of America, as their office manager, switchboard operator, and receptionist. That year, upon the birth of my first child, I promptly quit working to be a stay-at-home mom. At about that same time, my husband purchased what I considered an "overly fancy" printer for our home office. As it turned out, that printer led to my career in manuscript preparation! I had been doing odd jobs at home for the publisher (as I rocked my new baby), but then found out that I could do a job that one of the employees at the publishing company did! So I figured out how to use the appropriate software, learned how to use our over fancy printer, and have been my own boss ever since! (Of course, my degree in Family Studies is utilized daily, as a wife and a mother of two). I always try to remember to appreciate that being my own boss and working at home is an accomplishment that millions of women wish for . . . and I've been enjoying it thoroughly since 1993!*

For others, their career path takes shape when one day they are inspired by something going on around then, Carolyn Murray is one such example. She is Senior Editor of The Sun News, a McClatchy daily paper in Myrtle Beach, S.C., who also tells us how enamored she was of the English language.

*As a child, I loved telling stories and did well in English and writing classes. My eighth grade civics teacher first made me think of it as a career when he wrote "writing must be your forte" on an essay. But I didn't have the passion or imagination or patience to be a novelist or an English teacher. The newspapers of the day were full of Bob Woodward and Carl Bernstein's reporting on the Watergate scandal. So I went to the University of Missouri School of Journalism, graduated in 1976, and have worked as a reporter and editor ever since. I haven't yet brought down a president, but I still believe that providing information to the community that informs, enlightens and entertains is a great way to earn a living.*

Another interesting woman, who majored in advertising and marketing in college then landed an internship at Inc Magazine in New York City, is Pam Charlston De Grood, publisher of GS Magazine in Myrtle Beach, South Carolina.

*I fell in love with magazines because of that internship experience. Later, I got my first job with Yachting Magazine. A few years later I began selling advertising for some prestigious maga-*

*zines and used to say to myself, "One day I will start my own magazine." When I moved to Myrtle Beach I could see there was a niche here and that the public supported the idea of a magazine. It was a 24/7 endeavor but well worth it. GS Magazine is a lifestyle magazine and has been successfully publishing now for six years. A lifestyle magazine is a lifestyle in itself, and I could not have done it, or continue to do it, without the help of my husband and children.*

We have tried to present the facts about media careers, women (Chapter 2, Table 2.1) and mass media outlets—publishing houses, broadcast networks and radio and television stations, newspapers, magazines and movie studios. This is where women are needed the most, simply for variety. More minority women as well would help in diversity. Seeing through the lens of both men and women would add, we suggest, luster to media. Don't you think so?

## Finding Jobs in Mass Media

There are so many web sites that we assure you these are not all-inclusive. We do think they are good ones to review, however, for jobs in any mass media venue.

First, read the article in media job market called Eight Steps to Finding and Creating Work You Love written by Brian Kurth (www.media jobmarket.com/jobs/content_display/career-resource/diversity-workplace/ e3i669ba7401585bee09e614f9c13bf1358).

Second, follow Furth's suggestions in the above article before you get yourself into any of these job offers as an applicant.

Third, here is that promised list:

### Film and Television Industry

- MediaJobMarket offers Media Job Vine where you can find a list of jobs that includes writers at studios, web associates, account executives and others. (www.mediajobmarket.co/ jobs/index.jsp)
- Ross Reports claims to be the "pocket guide to the television and film industry." Their side bars indicate casting notices, television production, casting director searches, agent searches and more. It might be worth a subscription if you are serious

about the television/film industry. (www.backstage.com/bso/rossreports/about.jsp)

- Filmstaff.com is another site that appears to highlight jobs for actors, producers, camera operators, and others. www.filmstaff.com.

- This is a site of the California Chicano News Media Association that posts jobs across the country including producers, reporters, photographers, editors, graphic designers and more. www.ccnma.org/Television_jobs.htm

- This seems to be a hosting site for job portals. The site lists companies with job openings: Direct TV Latin America is advertising "Writer"; Paramount Pictures is advertising "Intern-Motion Pictures Music" www.entertainmentcareers.net

## Radio Industry

- This is an organization that focuses on both television and radio jobs. You can find job listings like radio training, music, sports broadcasting and lots more.
  http://tvandradiojobs. com/cgi-bin/classifieds/classified.cgi

- This is an organization devoted to radio talents (air talents). Their job positings include announcers, show commentators, disc jockeys in various radio broadcast markets.
  www.airtalents.com

- Here is the About.com site that does list jobs in media. For radio, they cite www.radioearth, www.radiojobs.net; *see* http://radio.about.com/library/blRadiojobOKs.htm

## Book Publishing Industry

- This site seems inclusive; they state they post jobs from over 300 publishers. The web page also sites Black Americans in publishing at www.baip.org.
  See this site at www.bookjobs.com

## Magazine Publishing

- This web site lists dozens of jobs around the country from sales to reporter to publicist to researcher and others. www.mediabistro.com/Magazine-Publishing-jobs.html

- The Magazine Publishers Association from which we can gather all types of stats about the industry has a job seekers link. They also post internship opportunities, Go to http://jobs.magazine.org

Olessa Pindak, the Beauty Editor for Natural Health Magazine says the following: "I do have one piece of advice: Never give up—jobs in this industry can be really hard to come by, but if you can just get your foot in the door—anywhere—real talent, hard work, and dedication will take you far."

## Newspaper Publishing

- There is a useful web site for the Southern Newspaper Publishers Association that lists various jobs in administrative, circulation, news, and more. www.snpa.org/index.cfm?fuseaction=CircuitAddOn.employmentjobs
- This site claims to be the nation's most comprehensive newspaper and media job banks. Go to www.newsjobs.com
- The Association of Newspaper Editors web page has a classified page with job listings from other organizations. This is probably the best web site we've seen for newspaper job resources. Go to www.asne.org/index.cfm?id=895

We offer one more site that is non-media specific. Where to Work for Women offers lots of information about media and entertainment jobs. www.wherewomenwanttowork.com

Of course you can always go to the corporate sites of the various media companies we have mentioned in this text. Each site (for example Gannett.com) lists job and internship listings. Take caution about paying any money at any web site you go to; don't give out too much personal information without thoroughly researching the site. See who they are and what they are before you post a resume or inquire about a job.

Good luck in job hunting!

# Further Reading About Women, Media and Issues

Creedon, Pamela J. (Ed.) (2006). *Women in Mass Communication.* 3rd ed., Newberry Park, Ca.: Sage Publications, Inc. This collection of essays pertains to three areas: research issues and feminist theory; perspectives on sexism and economic equity in mass communication industries; and faculty and students in mass communication programs.

Byerly, Carolyn M. and Karen Ross (2006). *Women and Media: a critical introduction.* London, UK: Blackwell Publishing. This text offers two parts: research on women and media (women as entertainment, images of women in news and magazines, women as audience and women and production; and women, media and the public sphere (chapters navigate from politics to media to politics to change agent to media enterprises).

Beasley, Maurine H. and Sheila J. Gibbons (2003). *Taking Their Place. A Documentary History of Women and Journalism.* (2nd ed). State College, PA: Strata Publishing, Inc. [This survey of collected writings begins in the Colonial Era and takes us to the present. It is loaded with excerpts of letters, stories and print material from various newspapers. The authors do a great job in offering resources pages separated by each medium and a timeline.].

Halper, Donna (2001). *Invisible Stars: A Social History of Women in American Broadcasting.* Armonk, NY: M.E.Sharpe [This is an inside look at radio and television; the author has some great personal experiences].

Holtzman, Linda (2000). *Media Messages: what film, television and popular music teach us about race, class, gender and sexual orientation.* Armonk, NY: M.E. Sharpe. [This text focuses on race, gender and sexual orientation and is very informative.].

Meyers, Marian (Ed.) (1999). *Mediated Women: Representations in Popular Culture.* Cresskill, NJ: Hampton Press, Inc. [Good research book; articles cover all venues of media.].

Lont, Cynthia (Ed.) (1995). *Women and Media: Content, Careers and Criticism.* Belmont, CA: Wadsworth. [Historical and contemporary material about women in media.].

*Table 11.1 Time Warner and Subsidiaries*

| | | | |
|---|---|---|---|
| **Time Warner** | Patricia Fili-Krushel, Exec. Vice Pres., Administration | Carol A. Melton, Exec. Vice Pres., Global Public Policy | |
| **AOL** | Tiane Mitchell Gordon, Sr. Vice Pres., Diversity & Inclusion | Tricia Primrose, Exec. Vice Pres., Corporate Communications | |
| **TW Cable** | Ellen East, Exec. Vice Pres., and Chief Communications Officer | Joan Gillman, Exec. Vice Pres., and President, Time Warner Cable Media Sales | Carol A. Hevey, Exec. Vice Pres., Operations, Carolina Region |
| **Time, Inc.** | Stephanie George, Exec. Vice Pres. | Sylvia Auton, Exec. Vice Pres. | Sheryl Tucker, Exec. Editor | Dawn Bridges, Sr. Vice Pres., Corporate Communications |
| **HBO** | Shelley Fischel, Exec. Vice Pres., Human Rsources | Carolyn Strauss, President | Sheila Nevins, President, HBO Documentry Films |

Compiled from corporate web pages.

(continued on next page)

## Table 11.1 Time Warner and Subsidiaries (continued)

| Turner Broadcast Systems | Louise Sams is Exec. Vice Pres., and General Counsel | Kelly Regal is Exec. Vice Pres. | | | |
|---|---|---|---|---|---|
| **Warner Bros.** | Susan Fleishman, Exec. Vice. Pres., Corporate Communications | Polly Cohen, President, Warner Independent Pictures | Hilary Estey McLoughlin, President, Telepictures Productions | Diane Nelson, President, Warner Premiere | Sue Kroll, President, Worldwide Marketing, Warner Bros., Pictures | Veronika Kwan-Rubinek, President, Distrbution, WB Pictures International |
| **Global Media** | Ann Brown, Sr. Vice Pres., Creative Strategy | Kristen O'Hara, Sr. Vice Pres., & Managing Director | | | |

Compiled from corporate web pages.

# Notes

1. Read the rest of this article, "Want to Get Video Seen? Think Context" at www.imediaconnection.com/content/13606.asp.

2. THR February 5, 2007. "Nick boosts environmental impact with Nicktropolis.

3. Ibid.

4. THR January 2007, Emerging platforms.

5. THR February 13-19, 2007, p. 7.

6. THR February 13-19, 2007, p. 7.

7. NPR.

8. You can access these blogs on www.internetevolution.com/.

# Index

# About the Authors

Lee Bollinger is a native of New Orleans, La., obtained her doctorate in journalism and mass communication from the University of South Carolina and is an associate professor in the Department of Communication at Coastal Carolina University. Her primary focus in teaching and in writing has been in magazines and newspapers within which she has published extensively. She likes to think of herself as a reporter "to the core" for it seems, she says, that her adult life is spent in searching for the facts all the time. For hobbies, she gets out in the garden, goes to the beach and attempts every now and then to paint, though she admits she can't paint a thing beyond flowers.

Carole O'Neill is an Emmy award winning producer/director who aired news, talk shows, documentaries and live specials on CBS, NBC and WB affiliates in Boston as well as on WGBH-TV, the Boston PBS station. After spending nearly twenty years as an Emerson College professor in the School of the Arts, she took early retirement, moved with her husband to Myrtle Beach and became a visiting professor at Coastal Carolina University. In addition to writing and television courses, she specializes in the entertainment world of Hollywood. In her leisure time, she and her husband, Jim, are movie buffs, attending two or three new ones each week. It gets expensive but it's a great tax write off.